Read Real NIHONGO

Japanese texts
for intermediate learners

JN090576

The Complete Guide to Japanese Systems

ぜんずかい　　にほん
全図解 日本のしくみ

Abe Naobumi
安部直文

Michael Brase = translator
マイケル・ブレーズ＝訳

IBC パブリッシング

装　　幀＝見増　勇介、関屋　晶子(ym design)
翻訳協力＝ Matt Treyvaud

本書は2022年に弊社から刊行された『全図解 日本のしくみ 増補改訂判』(安部直文著、マイケル・ブレーズ訳)を元に再構成したものです。

●音声一括ダウンロード●

本書の🔊マークの日本語の朗読音声(MP3形式)を下記URLとQRコードから無料でPCなどに一括ダウンロードすることができます。

https://ibcpub.co.jp/audio_dl/0788/

※ダウンロードしたファイルはZIP形式で圧縮されていますので、解凍ソフトが必要です。
※MP3ファイルを再生するには、iTunes (Apple Music) やWindows Media Playerなどのアプリケーションが必要です。
※PCや端末、ソフトウェアの操作・再生方法については、編集部ではお答えできません。付属のマニュアルやインターネットの検索を利用するか、開発元にお問い合わせください。

Audio Download

You can download the audio version (MP3 format) of this book in Japanese to your PC or other devices free of charge from the following URL and QR code:

https://ibcpub.co.jp/audio_dl/0788/

Please note the following:

* The downloaded files are compressed in ZIP format, so decompression software is required.
* To play MP3 files, applications such as iTunes (Apple Music) or Windows Media Player are required.
* The editorial team cannot answer questions about PC, device, or software operation and playback methods. Please consult the provided manual, search online, or reach out to the developer.

About the *Read Real NIHONGO* Series

Reading Sets You Free

The difficulty of reading Japanese is perhaps the greatest obstacle to the speedy mastery of the language. A highly motivated English speaker who wants to make rapid progress in a major European language such as Spanish, French or German need only acquire a grasp of the grammar and a smattering of vocabulary to become able to at least attempt to read a book. Thanks to a common alphabet, they can instantly identify every word on the page, locate them in a dictionary, and figure out—more or less—what is going on.

With Japanese, however, *kanji* ideograms make it infinitely harder to make the jump from reading with guidance from a teacher to reading freely by oneself. The chasm dividing the short example sentences of textbooks from the more intellectually rewarding world of real-world books and articles can appear unbridgeable. Japanese—to borrow Nassim Taleb's phrase—is an "Extremistan" language. *Either* you master two thousand *kanji* characters with their various readings to achieve breakthrough reading proficiency and the capacity for self-study *or* you fail to memorize enough *kanji*, your morale collapses, and you retire, tired of floating in a limbo of semi-literacy. At a certain point, Japanese is all or nothing, win or lose, put up or shut up.

The benefits of staying the course and acquiring the ability to read independently are, of course, enormous.

Firstly, acquiring the ability to study by yourself without needing a teacher increases the absolute number of hours that you can study from "classroom time only" to "as long as you want." If there is any truth to the theories about 10,000 hours of practice being needed to master any skill, then clearly the ability to log more hours of Japanese self-study has got to be a major competitive advantage.

Secondly, exposure to longer texts means that your Japanese input rises in simple quantitative terms. More Japanese *going into* your head means that, necessarily, more Japanese *stays in* your head! As well as retaining more words and idioms, you will also start to develop greater mental stamina. You will get accustomed to digesting Japanese in real-life "adult" portions rather than the child-sized portions you were used to in the classroom.

Thirdly, reading will help you develop tolerance for complexity as you start using context to help you figure things out for yourself. When reading a book, the process goes something like this: You read a sentence; should you fail to understand it first time, you read it again. Should it still not make sense to you, you can go onto the next sentence and use the meaning of that one to "reverse-engineer" the meaning of its predecessor, and so on. By doing this, you will become self-reliant, pragmatic and—this is significant—able to put up with gaps in your understanding without panicking, because you know they are only temporary. You will morph into a woodsman of language, able to live off the land, however it may be.

That is the main purpose of the *Read Real NIHONGO* series: to propel you across the chasm that separates those who read Japanese from those who cannot.

Furigana the Equalizer

Bilingual books have been popular in Japan since the 1990s. Over time, they have grown more sophisticated, adding features like comprehensive page-by-page glossaries, illustrations and online audio. What makes the *Read Real NIHONGO* series—a relative latecomer to the scene—special?

It all comes down to *furigana*. This is the first ever series of bilingual books to include *furigana* superscript above every single *kanji* word in the text. Commonly used in children's books in Japan, *furigana* is a tried-and-tested, non-intrusive and efficient way to learn to read *kanji* ideograms. By enabling you to decipher every word immediately, *furigana* helps you grasp the meaning of whole passages faster without needing to get bogged down in fruitless and demoralizing searches for the pronunciation of individual words.

By providing you with the pronunciation, *furigana* also enables you to commit new words to memory right away (since we remember more by sound than by appearance), as well as giving you the wherewithal to look them up, should you want to go beyond the single usage example on the facing English page. *Read Real NIHONGO* provides a mini-glossary at the foot of each page to help you identify and commit to memory the most important words and phrases.

Raw Materials for Conversation

So much for *furigana* and the language-learning aspect—now for the content. The books in this series are all about Japan, from its customs, traditions and cuisine to its history, politics and economy. Providing essential insights into what makes the Japanese and their society tick, every book can help you as you transition from ignorant outsider to informed insider. The information the books contain gives you a treasure trove of raw materials you can use in conversations with Japanese people. Whether you want to amaze your interlocutors with your knowledge of Japanese religion, impress your work colleagues with your mastery of party-seating etiquette and correct bowing angles, or enjoy a heated discussion of the relative merits of arranged marriages versus love marriages, *Read Real NIHONGO* is very much the gift that keeps on giving.

We are confident that this series will help everyone—from students to businesspeople and diplomats to tourists—start reading Japanese painlessly while also learning about Japanese culture. Enjoy!

Tom Christian
Editor-in-Chief
Read Real NIHONGO Series

はじめに

　本書は、主として外国の方々に日本という国や日本人の暮らしぶりを、できるだけシンプルにご紹介することを目的にしています。また、基本的な日本語学習のテキストとしての役割もあります。

　日本の社会制度や人々の生活は、国際化・情報化といった時流に合わせてめまぐるしく変化をし続けていますが、その底流には日本人のオリジナリティーともいうべき不変の精神性があるように思われます。実は日本を、日本人を正しく理解するためには、そうした精神性に眼を向けていただく必要があるのですが、それは本書の目的外です。

　あえて、その一端に触れるならば、日本人の精神性は「自然との一体化」を指向している点にあると言ってよいでしょう。例えば「芽(目)が出て、茎(口)が伸び、葉(歯)が開き、花(鼻)が咲いて、実(耳)が生る」といった、植物と人間の顔の部位の呼称の相似は、自然と一体であることを日本人が自覚していた表れとも考えられます。

　植物との関係で言えば、本来の日本は穀物・野菜を主にした食事、稲わら・イグサ・木材・紙などを材料にした建物や建具、木製の乗り物、綿や麻で織りあげた衣類、薬草を原料にした医薬品、そして燃料は炭・薪・菜種油というように、生活全般が光合成による"光エネルギー"で生育した植物で成り立っていました。植物から作ったものは、利用後は自然に還元でき、環境に悪影響を及ぼすことはありません。

　ところで、日本を訪れた外国の方々が一様に驚嘆するのは、自然の美しさと日本人の礼儀正しさだそうです。そして礼儀正しさは、しばしば人間に危害を及ぼす自然に対する「畏怖」に起因しているように思われます。

　このような日本人特有の精神性を踏まえつつ、本書を読んでいただければ幸いです。

2023年秋　安部直文

6

Preface

The aim of this book is to introduce Japan and the Japanese way of life as simply as possible to an audience consisting chiefly of people from other countries. The book can also serve a text while learning basic Japanese.

Japanese social systems and lifestyles continue to change rapidly in response to globalization and computerization, but a persistent undercurrent of unchanging Japanese psychology seems to remain—what might be called the originality of the Japanese people. The truth is that Japan and its people cannot be understood properly without examining this psychology, but that is beyond the scope of this book.

Nevertheless, it we were to touch briefly on this matter, we might point out the tendency in this Japanese psychology toward "unity with nature." For example, if we consider that the Japanese word for "eyes" (*me*) is homophonous with the word for "sprout," the word for "mouth" (*kuchi*) similar to the word for "stalk" (*kuki*), the word for "tooth" (*ha*) homophonous with the word for "leaf," the word for "nose" (*hana*) homophonous with the word for "flower," and the word for "nose" (*mimi*) similar to the word for "fruit" (*mi*), we might conclude that these parallels between the names for parts of a plant and for facial features suggest an awareness among the Japanese of their unity with nature.

On the topic of plants, Japan was originally characterized by diets chiefly of grains and vegetables; buildings and furniture made of materials like rice straw, rushes, wood, and paper; wooden vehicles; clothing woven of cotton and help; treatments for illness prepared from medicinal plants; and charcoal, wood, and rapeseed oil as fuel. In other words, every part of life depended on plants grown through "solar power" in the form of photosynthesis. Items made from plants can be returned to nature after they are used, with no negative effect on the environment.

However, what foreign visitors to Japan were united in admiration for was the country's natural beauty and the politeness of its people. And that politeness seems to me to be rooted in awe of nature, which so frequently brought disaster to humanity.

I hope that readers will consider the contents of this book in the context of the unique psychology of the Japanese people.

Abe Naobumi
Autumn 2023

Introduction
Four Key Words to Understanding Japan

<ruby>序章<rt>じょ しょう</rt></ruby> ニッポンを<ruby>読<rt>よ</rt></ruby>む
４つのキー・ワード

これだけはしっかり<ruby>押<rt>お</rt></ruby>さえておこう！
Let's Get This Right!

感染症のしくみ

◁))）　2019年に発生して世界的大流行（パンデミック）をもたらした新型コロナウイルス感染症は、日本にとってはスペイン風邪（スペイン・インフルエンザ）以来一世紀ぶりに爆発的流行をした感染症である。

　これに対して政府は当初「二類感染症相当」（閣議決定）としたが、すぐに一類感染症のみを対象とする「無症状者への適用」が付け加えられ、さらに「外出自粛要請」を行うことになった。（注）

　政府の対応の迷走は、右の表のように感染症に対する法律上の分類と制約のためで、すぐに有効な手を打てない原因もここにあるといえるだろう。

警戒レベル
Alert Level

フェーズ Phase **1**
ヒト感染のリスクが低い
Low risk of human infection

フェーズ Phase **2**
ヒト感染のリスクが高い
High risk of human infection

フェーズ Phase **3**
ヒトーヒト感染のリスクはないか、限定的
No or limited risk of person-to-person transmission

フェーズ Phase **4**
ヒトーヒト感染が増加している証拠がある
Evidence of increased person-to-person transmission

フェーズ Phase **5**
かなりの数のヒトーヒト感染の証拠がある
Evidence of considerable person-to-person transmission

Pandemic

（注）2023年5月8日、新型コロナウイルス感染症は「五類感染症」に移行した
On May 8, 2023, COVID-19 was reclassified as a "Class 5 infectious disease"

□感染症　infection, infectious disease
□爆発的流行　explosive outbreak
□相当　equivalent to
□閣議決定　cabinet decision

□無症状者　asymptomatic person
□〜を自粛する　refrain from
□分類　classification
□制約　restriction

The novel coronavirus infection broke out in 2019 and caused a global pandemic. This was the first explosive outbreak of an infectious disease in Japan since the Spanish flu (Spanish influenza) about a century ago.

In response, the government initially designated the disease as "equivalent to a Category 2 infectious disease" (by cabinet decision). Right away, "includes asymptomatic persons," which applies to only Category 1 infectious diseases, was added. In addition, it was decided to make a "request to refrain from going out."

The government's hesitant response was due to the legal classifications and restrictions on infectious diseases, as shown in the table below, and this is also the reason for the government's inability to take effective measures immediately.

法律上の分類と措置（抜粋）
Legal Categories and Measures (excerpts)

一類感染症 Category I InfectiousDiseases	エボラ出血熱、ペスト、ラッサ熱等 Ebola hemorrhagic fever, plague, Lassa fever, etc.	入院勧告、就業制限、消毒、交通制限、医療費公費負担 Hospitalization advisory, restrictions on work, disinfection, traffic restrictions, public funding for medical expenses
二類感染症 Category II InfectiousDiseases	ポリオ、結核、ジフテリア、SARS、コロナウイルス Polio, tuberculosis, diphtheria, SARS, coronavirus	入院勧告、就業制限、消毒、医療費公費負担 Hospitalization advisory, restrictions on work, disinfection, public funding for medical expenses
三類感染症 Category III InfectiousDiseases	コレラ、細菌性赤痢、O-157、腸チフス等 Cholera, bacillary dysentery, O-157, typhoid fever, etc.	就業制限、消毒 Restrictions on work, disinfection
四類感染症 Category IV InfectiousDiseases	主に動物を介してヒトに感染 Mainly infects humans via animals	消毒 Disinfection
五類感染症 Category V InfectiousDiseases	インフルエンザ、麻疹、風疹、百日ぜき、梅毒等 Influenza, measles, German measles, whooping cough, syphilis, etc.	発生動向調査 Infection surveillance
新型インフルエンザ等 H1N1 influenza, etc.	国民が免疫を獲得していないインフルエンザ Influenza from which the population has not acquired immunity	入院勧告、消毒、外出自粛要請等 Hospitalization advisory, disinfection, request to refrain from going out
新感染症 New infectious disease	ヒトからヒトへ感染し、危険性が極めて高い感染症 Infectious disease that can be transmitted from person to person and is extremely hazardous.	対応は担当大臣が都道府県知事に指導・助言 Minister in charge provides guidance and advice to the prefectural governors regarding response.

ニッポンを読む４つのキー・ワード

予防接種

1994年10月、「予防接種法」などの法律改正によって、予防接種のやり方が変わった。インフルエンザの予防接種の後遺症をめぐる判決で、国側が敗訴したことが引き金になって制度の見直しが行われたものだ。子供の予防接種は従来、集団接種を原則としてきたが、１人の医師が１時間ほどで100人前後の子供に接種をしなければならないため、予診がおろそかになり、それが副作用事故につながるおそれのあることが指摘されていた。現在、予防接種は家庭の判断で行う努力義務となっている。

子供の予防接種は、**原則として**保護者の判断で選択し、個別に医師から受ける

Children are now vaccinated individually at the discretion of the parent or guardian.

市区町村役所
Local government office

通知
Notification

費用支払い
Payment

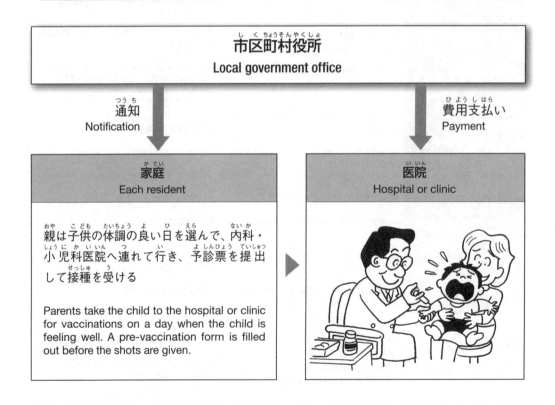

家庭
Each resident

親は子供の体調の良い日を選んで、内科・小児科医院へ連れて行き、予診票を提出して接種を受ける

Parents take the child to the hospital or clinic for vaccinations on a day when the child is feeling well. A pre-vaccination form is filled out before the shots are given.

医院
Hospital or clinic

□改正する revise　　　　□従来 in the past　　　　□原則として as a rule

□後遺症 aftereffect　　　□予診 pre-diagnosis

□引き金になる be triggered by　　□努力義務 use one's best effort

Vaccinations

In October 1994, various laws were revised to change the way that vaccinations in Japan are carried out. This change in the system was triggered by a suit brought against the government concerning the aftereffects of influenza vaccinations. Childhood vaccinations were typically carried out in groups, but in circumstances where one doctor would give around a hundred shots in an hour, it was almost impossible to make a pre-diagnosis, and this led to harmful aftereffects. Under the new system, parents are now encouraged to have their children vaccinated.

対象疾病
Illness

ジフテリア	Diphtheri
百日ぜき	Whooping cougha
ポリオ	Polio
麻疹	Measles
風疹	German measles
日本脳炎	Japanese encephalitis
結核	Tuberculosis
破傷風	Tetanus

2006年の法改正で、麻疹・風疹（MR）ワクチンの２回接種（１歳、小学校入学前１年間）が義務づけられた

Following a 2006 law revision, it became compulsory for children one year old and one year before entering elementary school to have a two-dose vaccination of MR (measles and German measles or rubella).

2021年2月に接種が始まった新型コロナウイルス感染症（COVID-19）の「mRNAワクチン」開発に貢献した一人が、ハンガリー出身の生化学者カタリン・カリコー博士（1955–）。国際科学技術財団は、2022年「日本国際賞」を授与した

Dr. Katalin Kalikó (1955–), a Hungarian biochemist, was one of the people who contributed to the development of the mRNA vaccine for the new coronavirus infection (COVID-19). Inoculations against it began in February 2021. The International Science Foundation awarded her the "Japan International Prize" for 2022.

自然災害対応のしくみ

02

2011年3月11日に起きた**東北地方太平洋沖地震**は、震度7、マグニチュード9.0という**観測史上最大**の巨大地震だった。さらに地震発生後に襲った大津波は高さ15メートル超のものもあり、東日本の**沿岸**地域に大被害を与えた。地震は主に**地殻**の破壊や**地層**のずれなどが原因で起きるが、今回の地震は太平洋の海底プレートの**沈下**によって起きた。

"**天災**は忘れた頃にやって来る"という言葉があるように、日々の備えと、**避難ルート**の確認が大事になる。

大災害が発生した場合は、「**災害対策基本法**」に基づき**緊急対策本部**が設置され、**応急対策**や災害復旧が行われる。住宅の被災は、①全壊、②大規模半壊、③半壊、④一部破損の4段階で判定され、大規模半壊以上については**支援金**が給付される。

ニッポンを読む4つのキー・ワード

□東北地方太平洋沖地震 The Earthquake Off the Pacific Coast of Tohoku
□震度 the Japanese seismic scale
□観測史上最大の the largest recorded
□沿岸 coast
□地殻 the earth's crust
□地層 strata
□ずれ slippage
□沈下 sinkage
□天災 disaster
□避難ルート evacuation route
□災害対策基本法 the Basic Act on Disaster Control Measures
□緊急対策本部 an Emergency Response Headquarters
□応急対策 emergency measure
□復旧 recovery
□支援金 relief fund

16

Response to Natural Disasters

The Earthquake Off the Pacific Coast of Tohoku of March 11, 2011, registered 7 on the Japanese seismic scale and had a magnitude of 9 on the MMS scale, making it the largest recorded earthquake in Japanese history. The following tsunami reached as much as 15 meters in height in some areas and spread massive destruction along the coast. Generally speaking, earthquakes occur due to destruction of the earth's crust and to the slippage of strata, but this earthquake was due to the sinkage of the Pacific plate.

As indicated by the saying, "Disasters come just when you have forgotten the last one," it is important to be always prepared and recheck evacuation routes.

When a catastrophe disaster occurs, an Emergency Response Headquarters is established according to the Basic Act on Disaster Control Measures, and emergency and recovery measures are implemented. Residential damage is divided into four categories: 1) totally destroyed, 2) major damage, 3) half destroyed, and 4) partially destroyed. For buildings suffering major damage or more, relief funds are distributed.

Four Key Words to Understanding Japan

ニッポンを読む4つのキー・ワード

緊急地震速報・津波情報
Earthquake Early Warnings and Tsunami Warnings

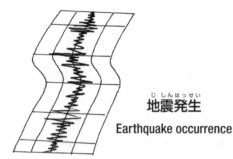

地震発生
Earthquake occurrence

気象庁
Meteorological Agency

直後
Immediately afterword

緊急地震速報 Earthquake Early Warning	1観測点による推定震源と規模 Estimated epicenter and magnitude from 1 seismometer

約5秒後
About 5 seconds later

緊急地震速報 Earthquake Early Warning	2〜3観測点による推定震源と規模 Estimated epicenter and magnitude from 2 to 3 seismometers

数10秒後
Several 10 of seconds later

緊急地震速報 Earthquake Early Warning	多数の観測点による推定震源と規模 Estimated epicenter and magnitude from many seismometers

2分以内
Within 2 minutes

緊急地震速報 Earthquake Early Warning	津波警報・注意報 Tsunami Warnings and Tsunami Advisories

規模の大きさ Size	震度階 級 Order of Magnitude	（M）マグニチュード （M）Magnitude
巨大地震 Great	7	M ≧ 8
大地震 Major	6強 6 or more	M ≧ 7
	6弱 6 or less	
中 地震 Moderate	5強 5 or more	7 > M ≧ 5
	5弱 5 or less	
小 地震 Light	4	5 > M ≧ 3
	3	
微小地震 Minor	2	3 > M ≧ 1
	1	
極微小地震 Micro	0	1 > M

◁))) 地震発生から約3分後に発表する「津波警報」の第一報では、予想される津波の高さを「巨大」や「高い」などと表現する。正確な地震の規模が分かったところで発表されるのが、津波の高さを5段階（1m、3m、5m、10m、10m超）で示した警報である

The first "tsunami warning" is issued about three minutes after an earthquake, and the height of the expected tsunami is described as "huge" or "high." The tsunami warning is issued when the exact magnitude of the earthquake is known, and indicates the height of the tsunami using five levels (1 m, 3 m, 5 m, 10 m, or over 10 m).

警戒宣言発令のプロセス
Earthquake Warning Process

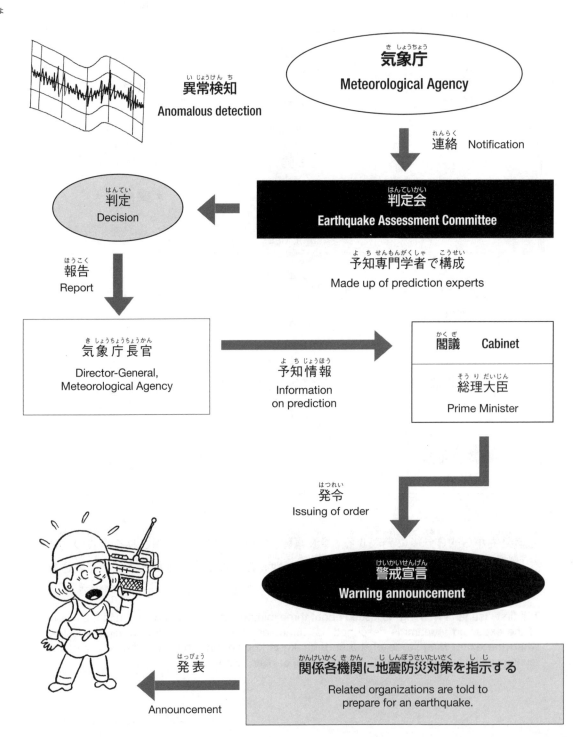

異常検知
Anomalous detection

気象庁
Meteorological Agency

連絡　Notification

判定
Decision

判定会
Earthquake Assessment Committee

予知専門学者で構成
Made up of prediction experts

報告
Report

気象庁長官
Director-General,
Meteorological Agency

予知情報
Information
on prediction

閣議　Cabinet

総理大臣
Prime Minister

発令
Issuing of order

警戒宣言
Warning announcement

発表
Announcement

関係各機関に地震防災対策を指示する
Related organizations are told to
prepare for an earthquake.

Four Key Words to Understanding Japan

警戒宣言とは法律に基づき行われる地震予知で、現在は東海地震に限定されている。観測で異常が検知された場合、地震注意情報または警戒宣言のいずれかが状況に応じて発表される。

Earthquake Warnings are earthquake predictions carried out on the basis of established law and are at present restricted to the Tokai region. When anomalous movements of the earth are detected, Earthquake Warnings or Advisories are issued.

医療救護
Medical Aid

被災地では、医師が応急的に死傷者に対して「トリアージ・タッグ」を付け、切り取ることで治療の優先度が識別できるようにする。

In disaster areas, medical workers attach triage tags to victims (both live and dead) as an emergency measure, and by the use of tear-offs indicate the priority of their injuries.

0	死亡群 Lost	黒 black
I	緊急治療群 Cannot wait	赤 red
II	準緊急治療群 Has to wait	黄 yellow
III	軽傷群 Can wait	緑 green

ニッポンを読む4つのキー・ワード

警戒レベルと取るべき行動
Alert Level and Actions to Take

豪雨などによる自然災害が多発するようになった近年、防災気象情報の周知徹底が求められている。特に市区町村が発令する「避難準備・高齢者等避難開始」は、逃げ遅れたために被災してしまう高齢者や体が不自由な人を優先して避難させよう

というものである

In recent years, natural disasters, such as torrential rains, have become more frequent, requiring thorough dissemination of weather information for disaster prevention. In particular, a local government's "preparation for evacuation/start of evacuation of the elderly, etc." plan is intended to prioritize the evacuation of the elderly and physically disabled who will be affected by the disaster if they are left behind.

警戒レベル Alert level	レベル 1 Level 1	レベル 2 Level 2
気象庁の情報 Information from the Meteorological Agency	早期注意情報 Early warning	大雨・洪水注意報 Heavy rain/Flood warning
		氾濫注意情報 Flood warning
自治体の情報 Local government information		
状況 Situation	気象状況悪化の恐れがある Weather conditions may worsen	気象状況の悪化 Worsening weather conditions
取るべき行動 Actions to take	災害への心構えを高める Increase disaster preparedness	自らの避難行動を確認する Confirm own evacuation plan

□豪雨 torrential rain　　　　□周知徹底 thorough dissemination

警戒レベルは1から順に危険度が高くなっていく。避難は高齢者や体が不自由な人はレベル3までに、それ以外の人はレベル4までに行う。レベル5では手遅れになる

The danger level begins at 1 and increases as the numbers rise. Elderly and disabled persons should evacuate by Level 3, and all others by Level 4. By Level 5, it is too late to evacuate.

全員避難してくださーい！

Please evacuate, everyone.

レベル Level 3	レベル Level 4	レベル Level 5
大雨・洪水警報 Heavy rain/Flood alert	土砂災害警戒情報 Landslide disaster alert	大雨特別警報 Heavy rain special alert
氾濫警戒情報 Flood alert	氾濫危険情報 Flood hazard	氾濫発生情報 Flood occurrence
高齢者等避難 Evacuation for the elderly, etc.	避難指示 Evacuation order	緊急安全確保 Emergency safety measures
災害発生の恐れがある Risk of disaster	災害発生の恐れが高い High risk of disaster	災害が発生または切迫 Disaster has occurred or is imminent
危険な場所から高齢者は避難する Elderly evacuate from danger zone	危険な場所から全員が避難する Evacuate everyone from danger zone	命の危険があるので、すぐに安全確保 Find immediate safety because lives are at risk

専守防衛_{せんしゅぼうえい}のしくみ

◁))) 第二次世界大戦の敗戦後(1946年11月)に公布された『日本国憲法』は、"戦争の放棄"をうたった世界に類のない憲法である。したがって他国に脅威を与える軍事力(軍隊)は持たず、自衛隊の名称が示すように"専守防衛"に徹することを国家理念としてきた。

　そして、この国家理念を堅持し続けてこられたのは「日米安全保障 条約」の存在があったからという点も無視するわけにはいかないだろう。実際、米国の同盟国としてその"核の傘"に守られた日本を攻撃しようという国はなかった。しかし、近年の緊迫した国際 情勢は日本の国家理念を揺るがせている。主に9条をめぐる「憲法改正」への動向も注視しなければならない(p.28参照)。

◁))) 米国がアジア・太平洋地域の安全保障上、地政学的な重要拠点と位置付けてきたのが沖縄である。在日米軍基地は130か所ほどあるが、その約74%が沖縄に集中していて総面積は沖縄本島の約18%を占める。米軍人や軍属などは「日米地位 協定」で身分が保証され、日本の法律が適用されないという問題がある

Okinawa has been positioned as an important geopolitical base for its security in the Asia-Pacific region. There are about 130 U.S. military bases in Japan, 74% of which are concentrated in Okinawa, accounting for about 18% of the total area of its main island. The status of U.S. military personnel and civilian employees is guaranteed under the Japan–U.S. Status of Forces Agreement, and there can be problems because Japanese law does not apply to them.

□公布する promulgate

□放棄 renounce

□類のない unique

□国家理念 national philosophy

□堅持する adhere to

□日米安全保障条約 US–Japan Security Treaty

□同盟国 ally

□核の傘 nuclear umbrella

□緊迫した tense

□揺るがす shake

□地政学的 geopolitical

□拠点 base

□軍属 military civilian employee

□適用する apply

Exclusively Defensive Posture

The Constitution of Japan, promulgated in November 1946 after Japan's defeat in World War II, is unique in the world, stating that Japan "renounces war." Therefore, Japan's national philosophy has been to have no military force that threatens other countries, and, as the name of the Self-Defense Forces indicates, to be committed to an "exclusively defensive posture."

It is impossible to ignore the fact that the existence of the Japan–US Security Treaty has enabled Japan to adhere to this national philosophy. In fact, no nation has ever attempted to attack Japan, which is protected by the nuclear umbrella as an ally of the United States. However, the tense international situation in recent years has shaken Japan's national ideals. The trend toward "constitutional revision," mainly with regard to Article 9, must also be closely watched. (See p.28)

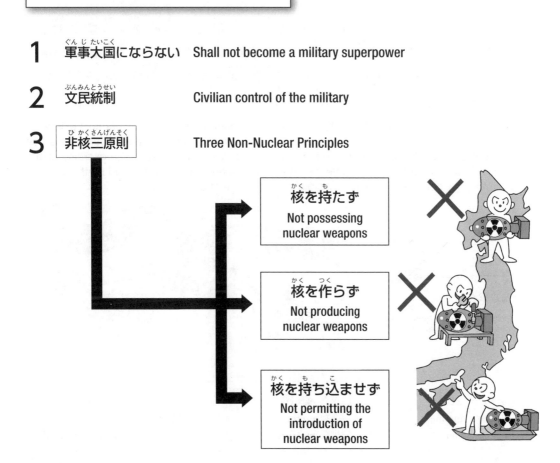

日本の防衛政策の原則
Principles of Japanese Defense Policy

1 軍事大国にならない　Shall not become a military superpower

2 文民統制　Civilian control of the military

3 非核三原則　Three Non-Nuclear Principles

核を持たず
Not possessing nuclear weapons

核を作らず
Not producing nuclear weapons

核を持ち込ませず
Not permitting the introduction of nuclear weapons

ニッポンを読む４つのキー・ワード

◁)) 有事の際の対応
Responses Emergency

有事とは「武力による紛争が生じている状態」を指す。具体的には、他国が武力攻撃をしてきたとき、またはその明白な危険が切迫しているとき、および事態が切迫し武力攻撃が予測されるときである。これらは国際法上でも認められている「個別的自衛権」の行使だが、武力攻撃が予測されるときの対応（反撃）については明確ではない

An emergency refers to a situation in which armed conflict is occurring. Specifically, it is when another country has launched an armed attack, or when there is an imminent and obvious danger of such an attack, or when an armed attack is predicted due to the situation. These are the instances when the exercise of the "right of individual self-defense" are recognized under international law, but it is not clear how to respond (counterattack) when an armed attack is anticipated.

◁)) 憲法９条のもとで許される武力行使
Use of Force Permitted Under Article 9 of the Constitution

上記の「個別的自衛権」に加え、日本と密接な関係にある他国（主に米国）に対する武力攻撃によって日本の存立が危ぶまれる事態になったときは、必要最小限度の武力行使ができる。いわゆる国際法上の「集団的自衛権」の発動だが、2014年の閣議決定で"自衛の措置として憲法上許容される"とした

In addition to the "right of individual self-defense" mentioned above, when Japan's existence is threatened by armed attacks against other countries with which Japan has close ties (mainly the United States), the minimum necessary force can be used. The exercise of the so-called right of collective self-defense under international law was decided by the Cabinet in 2014 to be "constitutionally permissible as a measure of self-defense."

日本を守る米軍への第三国による攻撃など

Attacks by third countries on U.S. forces defending Japan, etc.

□紛争 conflict　　　　□存立 existence　　　　□許容される permissible

□切迫した imminent　　□発動 exercise　　　　□放置する left unchecked

□事態 situation　　　　□措置 measure　　　　□〜とみなされる be deemed

有事につながる恐れのある事態への対応
Responding to Situations That May Lead to Emergencies

日本の存立が危ぶまれる事態ではないが、他国で起きている紛争を放置しておくと日本有事につながる恐れがあるとみなされるときは「後方支援活動」を行う。これには補給、輸送、医療などに加え、弾薬の提供（武器は不可）を含む。また、現地国の同意があれば外国（戦闘が行われている現場以外）での活動も可能

When a conflict in another country is deemed to have the potential to lead to an emergency in Japan if left unchecked, even though the existence of Japan is not threatened, "logistical support activities" will be conducted. This includes supply, transportation, medical care, etc., as well as the provision of ammunition (but not weapons). With the consent of the local country, activities in foreign countries (other than those where fighting is taking place) are also possible.

グレーゾーン事態　　"gray zone" situations

日本の領海内の離島に不審船がやってきた場合、対応するのは警察や海上保安庁である。だが、その集団が重武装をしていて取締まれないときは……。武力攻撃を受けたわけではないが、警察権の行使（治安出動）では対処が困難なケースを「グレーゾーン事態」という。自衛権の行使（防衛出動）には、原則として国家の意思による「組織的・計画的な武力行使」であると認定される必要がある

If a suspicious ship comes to a remote island in Japan's territorial waters, it is the police and the Japan Coast Guard that respond. However, when the group is heavily armed and cannot be controlled....Cases in which there is no armed attack but it is difficult to deal with the situation through the exercise of police power (public security operations) are called "gray zone" situations. The exercise of the right of self-defense (defense operations) requires, in principle, that the situation be recognized as an "organized and planned use of force" by the will of the state.

☐ 後方支援 logistical support
☐ 補給 supply
☐ 弾薬の提供 provision of ammunition
☐ 領海 territorial water
☐ 不審船 suspicious ship
☐ 海上保安庁 Japan Coast Guard
☐ 治安 public security
☐ 認定する recognize

27

憲法改正のしくみ

ニッポンを読む４つのキー・ワード

◁ッ)) 『日本国憲法』は、法治国家・日本の根幹の法律である。そのために憲法改正は、他の法律の場合よりもはるかに厳しい規則がされている。たとえば、憲法改正には、衆・参両議院の総議員の３分の２の賛成で国会が発議し、国民投票で有権者の過半数の賛成がなければならない（第96条）のである。これを「憲法の最高法規性」といっているが、最終的には国民投票で採決するところに、憲法ゆえの面目がある。もし国会の発議によって国民投票が実施された場合には、有権者の過半数以上の賛成があれば憲法は改正され、公布されることになる。憲法改正の問題は久しく論議されてきたところだが、最終的には国民がその是非を決定するしくみになっているのだ。

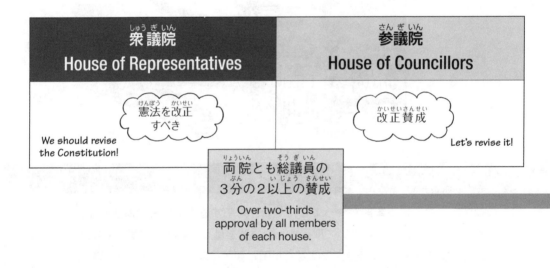

◁ッ)) 2010年５月に施行された「憲法改正手続法」では、衆議院100名以上、参議院50名以上の賛成で国会に発議できるとしている。しかし、最終的に改正には有権者の過半数以上の賛成が必要になる

The Constitutional Amendment Procedural Law enacted in May 2010 holds that revision can be brought up for discussion and resolution in the Diet with 100 or more Representatives and 50 Councillors voting in favor. However, a majority of voters is required for the final revision.

世論調査では、90年代以降は賛成が反対より上回っている

According to opinion polls, supporters of constitutional revision have outnumbered opponents since the early 1990s.

Revision of the Constitution

Since the Constitution of Japan is the country's basic law, any revision is subject to much stricter restrictions than are other laws. As stated in Article 96, amendments must be approved by two-thirds of both houses of the Diet and by a majority of the voters in a national election. The Constitution is the highest of all laws, and its main characteristic is that the final decision on amendments is left to the popular vote. If the Diet decides to hold a vote on a constitutional revision and the voters approve it by a simple majority, then the Constitution will be revised and promulgated. The question of whether to revise the Constitution has been debated for many years, and ultimately it is the people who will decide whether or not to do so.

□ 法治国家 constitutional state
□ 根幹の法律 basic law
□ 衆・参両議院 both houses of the Diet
□ 発議する propose
□ 国民投票 national referendum

□ 面目 dignity
□ 公布される be promulgated
□ 久しく for many years
□ 是非 whether or not to do so

法律制定のプロセス
The Legislative Process

法律案
Legislative bill

内閣提出法案
Cabinet-sponsored bill

議員立法
Diet member introduces legislation

閣議決定
Cabinet decision

法律案を発議するには、一定の条件（右ページ）が必要

To introduce a bill, a fixed procedure is followed (see page on right).

国会審議
Diet deliberations

議長は法律案を関連の委員会に付託し、審査をしてもらう。その後、本会議で審議をする

The speaker refers the bill to a relevant committee for examination. This is followed by deliberation by a plenary session.

議長 Speaker or President

- □ 付託する refer (to)
- □ 審査 examination
- □ 審議 deliberation
- □ 法律案の発議 moving a bill
- □ 所属する belong
- □ 認証する certify
- □ 施行する implement
- □ 両院協議会 joint committee of both houses
- □ 開催要求 request for holding

法律案を国会に提出できるのは、内閣と議員である。議員の場合は、**法律案の発議**といい、**所属する**議院に提出する。しかし、議員は一人では提出できず、衆議院では20人以上、参議院では10人以上の議員の賛成が必要になる。さらに予算のともなうものであれば、それぞれ50人以上、20人以上が必要である

Only the Cabinet and a Diet member can propose laws to the Diet. In the case of Diet members, they propose the legislation to the House to which they belong; this is called "moving a bill." However, a single member cannot move a bill. In the House of Representatives, 20 or more supporters are needed, and 10 in the House of Councillors. Moreover, if budgetary considerations are involved, then 50 and 20 favorable votes are needed, respectively.

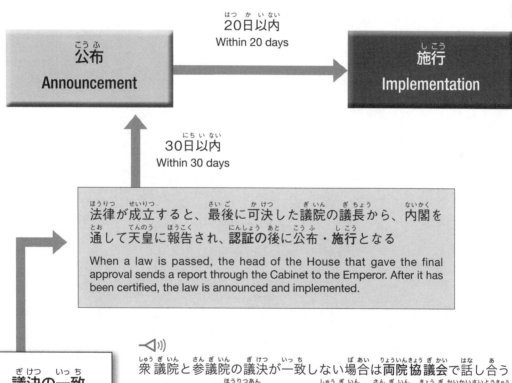

20日以内
Within 20 days

公布
Announcement

施行
Implementation

30日以内
Within 30 days

法律が成立すると、最後に可決した議院の議長から、内閣を通して天皇に報告され、認証の後に公布・施行となる

When a law is passed, the head of the House that gave the final approval sends a report through the Cabinet to the Emperor. After it has been certified, the law is announced and implemented.

議決の一致
Agreement between the Two Houses

衆議院と参議院の議決が一致しない場合は**両院協議会**で話し合うことになるが、法律案については衆議院が参議院の**協議会開催要求**を拒むことができる

When the Houses of Representatives and Councillors cannot reach agreement, deliberations are held between the two Houses. However, in the case of a legislative bill, the House of Representatives can refuse the House of Councillor's call for deliberation.

Chapter 1
Politics and Legislation

第1章 政治・司法

複雑なしくみをはっきりつかもう！
Let's Understand the Inner Workings

05

◁))　日本の選挙制度は衆議院と参議院に大別され、それぞれ次の見開きページのような選出方法によって行われる。しかし、制度自体については各選挙区間の1票の格差をめぐる有権者側からの違憲訴訟や、政党や派閥のエゴむき出しの選挙制度改革などが問題視されている。

　今の日本には国民のために働いてくれるたくさんの国会議員が必要だが、それにしても、米国の国会議員（上・下院）535名に比べてみても、総人口が3分の1ほどの日本の713名（2023年時点）は多すぎる。

□選挙制度　electoral system
□見開きページ　double spread
□1票の格差　the different value of votes

□違憲訴訟　lawsuit challenging the constitutionality
□改革　reform
□国会議員　Diet member

National Elections

Japan's electoral system is basically divided between the House of Representatives and the House of Councillors, each of which is elected using the methods shown on the following double spread. Lawsuits challenging the constitutionality of the different values of votes from different districts, and self-interested proposals for election reform put forth by political parties and factions are viewed as problem areas.

Japan needs a large number of Diet members to work for the people. Even so, the 713 members of the Diet in Japan (as of 2023), is far too many compared with the 535 members of the Congress (upper and lower houses) in the United States since Japan has only about one-third of America's population.

政治・司法
せいじ
しほう

国政選挙
こくせいせんきょ
National Elections

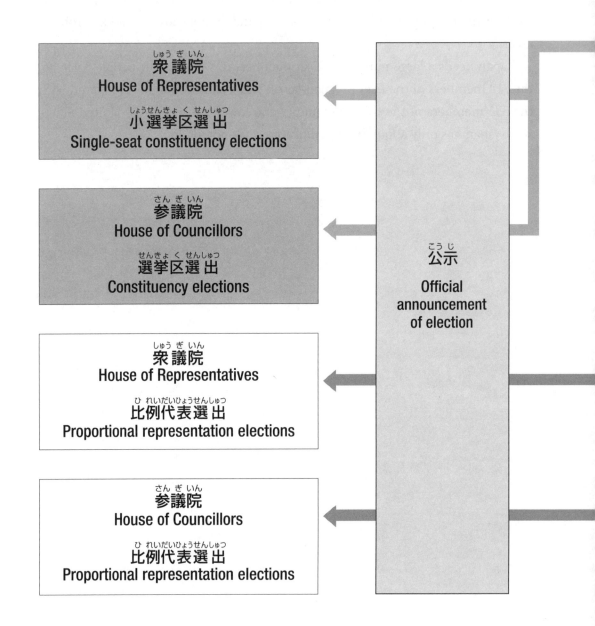

衆議院
しゅうぎいん
House of Representatives

小選挙区選出
しょうせんきょくせんしゅつ
Single-seat constituency elections

参議院
さんぎいん
House of Councillors

選挙区選出
せんきょくせんしゅつ
Constituency elections

衆議院
しゅうぎいん
House of Representatives

比例代表選出
ひれいだいひょうせんしゅつ
Proportional representation elections

参議院
さんぎいん
House of Councillors

比例代表選出
ひれいだいひょうせんしゅつ
Proportional representation elections

公示
こうじ
Official announcement of election

□議会 assembly
□邦人 Japanese
□指名する nominate
□任命する appoint
□国民審査 popular review

都道府県選挙管理委員会
Prefectural Election Management Councils

4名の委員は議会が選ぶ（任期は4年）

Four members, chosen by prefectural assemblies, serve four-year terms.

選挙権
Right to vote

満18歳以上の日本人と外国在住邦人（登録制）

Japanese citizens 18 years of age or older, including those living abroad who are registered.

満18歳以上

18 or older

中央選挙管理委員会
Central Election Management Council

5名の委員（任期は3年）

Five members serving three-year terms.

被選挙権
Right to hold office

Member of House of Councillors 30 or older

参議院議員 満30歳以上

衆議院議員 満25歳以上

Member of House of Representatives 25 or older

委員は国会が、国会議員以外の人を指名し、内閣総理大臣が任命する

Council members are nominated by the Diet from among people outside the Diet, and they are appointed by the Prime Minister.

◁))

中央選挙管理委員会は、最高裁判所裁判官の国民審査および憲法改正に関する国民投票の事務も行う

The Central Election Management Council also handles popular reviews of the Supreme Court and national votes on constitutional reform.

政治・司法

議員選出のしくみ
How Diet members are elected

衆議院
House of Representatives

小選挙区選出
Single-seat constituencies

都道府県ごとに2～25の選挙区に分けて議員を選出

Between 2 and 25 Diet members are chosen by each prefecture.

289名
289 members

比例代表選出
Proportional representation

全国を11のブロックに分け、7～33名の議員を選出。任期は4年だが、解散によって資格を失う

The country is divided into 11 blocks, each of which chooses between 7 and 33 Diet members. They are elected to four-year terms, but they lose their seats when the Diet is dissolved.

176名
176 members

急激な人口移動によって、地域間での1票の重みに格差があり、これは憲法違反ではないかという有権者からの訴訟に対して、最高裁は3倍以上の格差の是正を求める判断を下している

Due to rapid population shifts, a gap has appeared in the value of one vote between different districts, and voters filed a suit saying that this was unconstitutional. The Supreme Court ruled a gap of three times or greater to be unconstitutional.

A gap of over three times is unconstitutional. Revise it!

Supreme Court

最高裁

3倍以上の格差は違憲状態です改正せよ！

□解散する dissolve   □訴訟 suit   □最高裁 Supreme Court

参議院
House of Councillors

選挙区選出
Prefectural voting

全国を都道府県ごとに47選挙区に分けて議員を選出(地方区)

Members of the upper house are chosen from 47 districts, one for each prefecture.

148名
148 members

比例代表選出
Proportional representation

個人名と政党名を併用した投票方式で、得票数の多い順に当選者が決まる

Voters cast ballots for individual candidates and political parties in a combined format, with those elected being decided in the order of greatest number of votes.

100名
100 members

任期は6年で、3年ごとに半数を改選
Councillors serve six-year terms. Every three years, elections are held for half of the seats.

米国連邦議会
United States of America

アメリカと比べてみると……

Let's compare it with the United States

下院
House of Representatives
435名
435 members

上院
Senate
100名
100 members

各州の人口に比例した小選挙区制を採用。任期2年

Single-member districts are allocated according to the population of the states. The term of office is two years.

各州から2名ずつ選出し、2年で3分の1を改選。任期6年

Two Senators are chosen from each state to serve six-year terms. Every two years, elections are held for one-third of the seats.

06

政治・司法
せいじ　しほう

◁))　国会は、法治国家である日本の立法府であり、国権の最高機関である。国会は、衆議院と参議院の二院制をとっていて、両院の審議・議決を経てはじめて国事が決定するしくみになっている。

国会が開かれるのは、年1回1月に召集される通常国会、緊急を要する重要事項を審議する臨時国会、総選挙後に召集される特別国会の3つのケースである。

国会議事堂
こっかいぎじどう
The Diet Building

議事堂は1936年に完成し、左右対称。向かって右が参議院

The Diet Building was completed in 1936. It has a symmetrical design. The House of Councillors is on the right side.

中央の塔の高さは
65.45メートルある

The central tower of the Diet Building is 65.45 meters tall.

衆議院
しゅうぎいん
House of Representatives

参議院
さんぎいん
House of Councillors

両院協議会
りょういんきょうぎかい
Joint committee of both houses

□ 法治国家　constitutional state

□ 立法府　legislative body

□ 国事　matters of state

□ 通常国会　ordinary session

□ 臨時国会　extraordinary session

The Diet

Japan is a constitutional state with a bicameral Diet as its supreme legislative body. Matters of state are decided only with the Diet's deliberation and determination. The Diet goes in session one time a year in January, which is called an ordinary session.

Extraordinary sessions are called to discuss urgent matters, and special sessions are held after general elections.

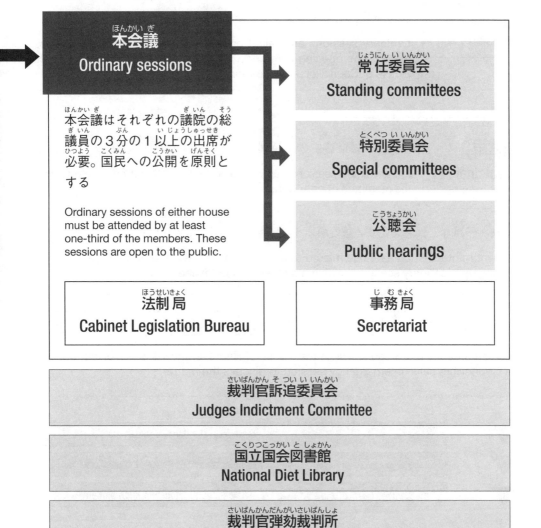

本会議（ほんかいぎ）
Ordinary sessions

本会議はそれぞれの議院の総議員の３分の１以上の出席が必要。国民への公開を原則とする

Ordinary sessions of either house must be attended by at least one-third of the members. These sessions are open to the public.

常任委員会（じょうにん いいんかい）
Standing committees

特別委員会（とくべつ い いんかい）
Special committees

公聴会（こうちょうかい）
Public hearings

法制局（ほうせいきょく）
Cabinet Legislation Bureau

事務局（じ む きょく）
Secretariat

裁判官訴追委員会（さいばんかん そ つい い いんかい）
Judges Indictment Committee

国立国会図書館（こくりつこっかい と しょかん）
National Diet Library

裁判官弾劾裁判所（さいばんかんだんがいさいばんしょ）
Judges Impeachment Court

議事堂に近接する議員会館は衆議院２棟、参議院１棟で、議員専用の事務室がある。家賃・水道光熱費・電話代（都内）はタダ。議事堂とは地下道で連結している

There are two House of Representatives buildings and one House of Councillors building adjacent to the Diet building, with offices for the exclusive use of members of the House of Councillors. Rent, utilities, and telephone charges (in Tokyo) are free. The buildings are connected to the Capitol Building by an underground passageway.

政治・司法

国会の種類
Diet Sessions

通常国会
Ordinary
sessions

年1回、1月に召集される国会で、開会式は天皇臨席のもと、参議院議場で行われ、会期は150日間

Ordinary sessions are called once a year in January. The Emperor attends the opening ceremony, which is held in the chamber of the House of Councillors. The session lasts 150 days.

臨時国会
Extraordinary
sessions

内閣または両議院の総議員の4分の1以上の要求で召集される国会

Extraordinary sessions can be called by the Cabinet or by one-fourth of the members of both Houses.

外交・予算など緊急を要する重要事項を審議する。2回まで会期延長ができる

Urgent matters, such as those related to foreign relations and the budget are discussed during extraordinary sessions, which may be extended twice.

衆議院の解散中に緊急事態が起きた場合は参議院が「緊急集会」を開いて審議する

If an emergency matter arises while the House of Representatives is dissolved, the House of Councillors calls an emergency session to discuss the matter.

| 総選挙 | General election |

| 参院閉会 | Adjournment of House of Councillors |

| 衆院解散 | Dissolution of House of Representatives |

特別国会
Special sessions

総選挙から30日以内に召集される国会

Special sessions are held within 30 days of general elections.

内閣総理大臣の指名をまず行う。2回まで会期延長ができる

Special sessions begin with the designation of the Prime Minister. They may be extended twice.

衆議院の優越事項
House of Representatives

衆議院と参議院が異なった議決をした場合は、両院協議会で話し合いが行われるが、それでもまとまらないときは、衆議院の議決が参議院の議決に優先して国会の議決となる

If the two Houses reach different decisions, a joint committee is formed to work out a compromise. If a middle ground cannot be found, the decision of the House of Representatives takes precedence in the case of:

- 法律案
- 予算案
- 条約の承認
- 内閣総理大臣の指名
- 内閣不信任→解散（衆議院のみ）

- Proposed legislation
- Budgets
- Approval of treaties
- Appointment of the Prime Minister
- No-confidence votes, and the dissolution of the House of Representatives

参議院は衆議院の行き過ぎを抑える

One of the House of Councillors' functions is to encourage members of the House of Representatives to take a balanced approach.

If worst comes to worst, we may force our decisions through regardless of you.

いざとなったら強行採決も辞さないぞ！

良識をもって行動してください。よ

I wish you would show better sense.

House of Representatives 衆議院

参議院 House of Councillors

芸能人やスポーツ選手出身議員は、通称名（芸名）による院内活動が認められている

Former entertainers and athletes are allowed to use their stage or professional names in the Diet.

□臨席する attend　　□総選挙 general election　　□通称名（芸名）stage or professional name

07

国会審議のしくみ

政治・司法

国会で審議される議案には、国会議員が提出するもの、委員会が提出するもの、**内閣**(関係大臣)が**提出する**ものがある。提出議案は、そのまま本会議で審議するのではなく、**議長**がその議案に関係する委員会に**付託する**。2つ以上の委員会にまたがる場合もあり、これを**連合審査会**という。委員会で充分に調査や審査を行った後に、はじめて本会議で審議される。

このプロセスは、衆議院と参議院の両院で同様に行われる。委員会を開催するには委員の半数以上の出席が必要で、その議決は出席委員の過半数の多数決による。委員は各党の議員数に**比例した**配分がされるが、委員長は**採決**に加われない。ただし**可否同数**のときは、委員長が決定する。

□内閣 Cabinet
□提出する submit
□議長 House speaker or president
□付託する assign

□連合審査会 joint committee
□比例する proportional
□採決 voting
□可否同数 equal number of votes

Diet Deliberations

Bills considered by the Diet can be submitted by individual members, committees, or Cabinet members. When a bill is submitted, it is not considered immediately by the full Houses, but is assigned by the House speaker or president to a committee. If the matter concerns more than one committee, it is considered by a joint committee. Only after the committee has studied and discussed the proposal thoroughly is it sent to the full House.

This process is the same in both the House of Representatives and the House of Councillors. At least half of the committee members must be present for a committee to meet, and the support of over half of the attending members is required for a bill to be approved by a committee. The number of committee members is proportional to each political party. The committee chairperson votes only to break ties.

政治・司法

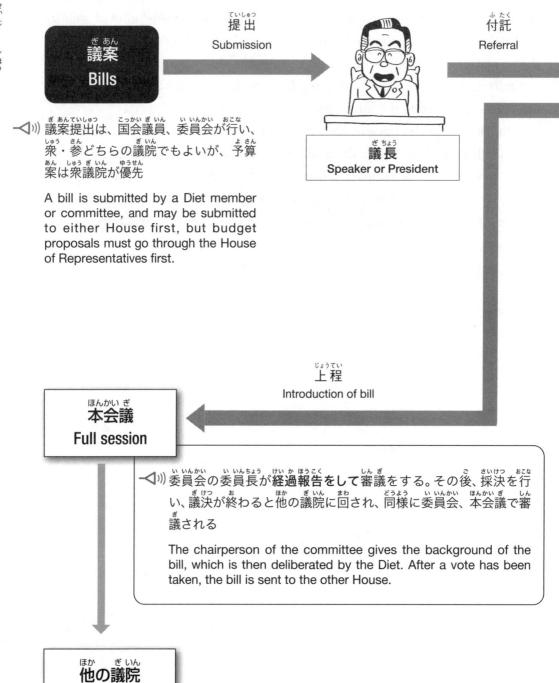

提出
Submission

付託
Referral

議案
Bills

議長
Speaker or President

◁)) 議案提出は、国会議員、委員会が行い、衆・参どちらの議院でもよいが、予算案は衆議院が優先

A bill is submitted by a Diet member or committee, and may be submitted to either House first, but budget proposals must go through the House of Representatives first.

上程
Introduction of bill

本会議
Full session

◁)) 委員会の委員長が**経過報告**をして審議をする。その後、採決を行い、議決が終わると他の議院に回され、同様に委員会、本会議で審議される

The chairperson of the committee gives the background of the bill, which is then deliberated by the Diet. After a vote has been taken, the bill is sent to the other House.

他の議院
Other house

委員会
Committee

常任委員会
Standing committees

国会に常時設けられている委員会で、衆議院に17、参議院に17ある。議員は少なくともひとつの委員会に所属しなければならない

Each House has permanent standing committees. The House of Representatives has 17 standing committees and the House of Councillors 17. Each Diet member must belong to at least one committee.

特別委員会
Special committees

会期ごとにそれぞれの議院で必要と認められた時に設置される。議案の議決後に消滅する

Special committees are established as necessary in each House for the current Diet session. The committees are dissolved after they have reached decisions on the bills they were considering.

審査
Deliberation process

▼ 趣旨説明（議案提出者）
Explanation of bill's main points
(by person who submitted the bill)

▼ 質疑（必要なら公聴会）
Question and answer time
(in public hearings when necessary)

▼ 討論　Debate

▼ 裁決　Vote

☐ 経過報告をする　give a background
☐ 常時設けられている　permanent standing
☐ 所属する　belong to

☐ 会期ごと　each session
☐ 設置される　be established

08

議案採決のしくみ

政治・司法

　委員会で審査された議案は、**本会議へ上程**される。そこで議院としての最終意思を決定するため、出席議員に賛否の意思表示を求める。これを採決という。本会議での採決の方法には3通りあって、ほぼ全員が賛成とみられる議案については議長が「ご**異議**ありませんか?」と問いかけ、「異議なし」の発声で**可決成立する**。賛否の数がある程度予想される場合は、議長が賛成議員に起立をさせ採決をする。重要法案などでは、**記名投票**という方法で、賛成は白票、反対は青票である。

　本会議は、議院の総議員の3分の1以上の出席により開催され、公開が原則。採決は、憲法改正や特別な議事以外は、出席議員の過半数の賛成により可決する。

□本会議 the full House
□上程する send
□異議 objection
□可決成立する the bill is passed
□記名投票 ballot with one's name on it

Passing of Bills

Bills that have been discussed in committee are then sent to the full House, where the members present make their final decision on whether or not to pass the bill. Bills may be passed in three ways. If nearly all members are likely to agree, the Speaker or President asks, "Are there any objections?" The members reply "No objection" and the bill is passed. If some disagreement is expected, the members who support the bill are told to stand. For especially important legislation, the members cast ballots with their names on them. Yes votes are on white ballots and no votes on blue.

Full sessions must be attended by at least one-third of the members and are open to the public. Except for constitutional revisions and other special matters, all decisions require a simple majority vote.

本会議
Full session

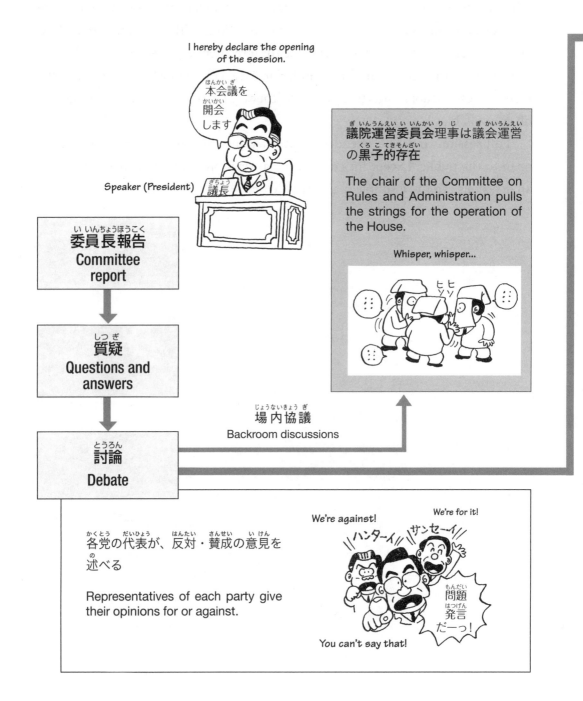

I hereby declare the opening of the session.

本会議を開会します

Speaker (President)　議長

委員長報告
Committee report

質疑
Questions and answers

討論
Debate

議院運営委員会理事は議会運営の黒子的存在

The chair of the Committee on Rules and Administration pulls the strings for the operation of the House.

Whisper, whisper...

場内協議
Backroom discussions

各党の代表が、反対・賛成の意見を述べる

Representatives of each party give their opinions for or against.

We're against!　ハンターイ

We're for it!　サンセーイ

問題発言だーっ!

You can't say that!

□議院運営委員会　the Committee on Rules and Administration
□黒子的存在　one who pulls the strings

採決
Adoption

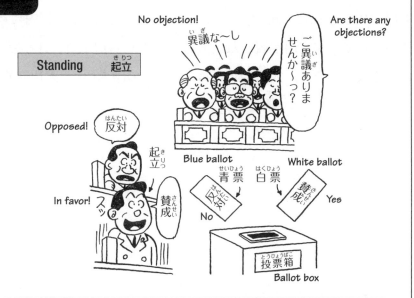

参議院は押しボタンによる電子式投票を採用

The House of Representatives has adopted an electronic voting system using buttons.

通常の議案については、出席議員の過半数で可決

Regular bills can be approved by a majority of the members present.

同数の場合は、議長が決定

In the case of a tie, the Speaker or President casts the tie-breaking vote.

他院の議長に送付する

Sent to head of other House.

09

政治・司法

内閣は**閣僚（国務大臣）によって構成され**、人選は総理大臣が決定権をもつ。しかし、近年は、**派閥や連立する他党にポスト配分されるのが常態になっている**。国務大臣は定数14だが、必要に応じ3名まで増やすことができる。

省の大臣は**主任大臣**と位置づけられ、この他に**無任所大臣、内閣府特命大臣**が任命される。総理大臣は**総理府**の主任大臣で、府内には内閣の**補助機関**として**内閣官房**が置かれ、その長である**官房長官**は国会議員から選出される大臣である。大臣の下には2〜3名の**副大臣**や、**大臣政務官**が置かれ、いずれも国会議員が就任する。

□閣僚 cabinet minister

□国務大臣 minister of state

□〜によって構成される consist of

□派閥 political faction

□連立する他党 allied party

□常態になる become the norm

□省 ministry

□主任大臣 responsible minister

□無任所大臣 minister without portfolio

□内閣府特命大臣 cabinet office minister

□総理府 prime minister's office

□補助機関 auxiliary agency

□内閣官房 cabinet secretariat

□官房長官 chief cabinet secretary

□副大臣 vice minister

□大臣政務官 parliamentary secretary

Forming a Cabinet

The cabinet consists of cabinet ministers (ministers of state) who are selected by the prime minister. Recently, it has become the norm for ministers to be appointed to posts depending on political faction or allied party. There are 14 Ministers of State, but up to three can be added if necessary.

A minister in charge of a ministry is classified as a responsible minister. In addition, there are also ministers without portfolio and cabinet office ministers extraordinary. The prime minister is the responsible minister for the prime minister's office, and within that office is placed the cabinet secretariat as an auxiliary agency, which is headed by the chief cabinet secretary, who is selected from among the diet members. Beneath each minister are two or three vice ministers and parliamentary secretaries, all of whom are diet members.

政治・司法

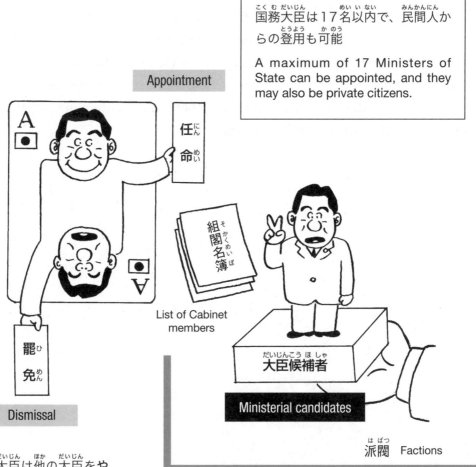

Appointment

任命

国務大臣は17名以内で、民間人からの登用も可能

A maximum of 17 Ministers of State can be appointed, and they may also be private citizens.

組閣名簿

List of Cabinet members

大臣候補者

Ministerial candidates

罷免

Dismissal

派閥 Factions

総理大臣は他の大臣をやめさせる権限がある

The Prime Minister has the power to force other ministers to resign.

総理大臣は任期の定めがなく、本人が辞意を表明しない限り、やめさせることは困難

The prime minister's term of office is not fixed, and unless he resigns of his own accord, he cannot easily be forced out of office.

□やめる resign
□〜させる権限 power to force

□任期 term of office
□辞意を表明する express one's resignation

衆議院
しゅう ぎ いん
House of
Representatives

・信任決議不成立　Failure of confidence vote
しんにんけつ ぎ ふ せいりつ
・不信任が議決　Vote of no-confidence
ふ しんにん　　 ぎ けつ

内閣総辞職
ないかくそう じ しょく
Resignation of entire
Cabinet

解散
かいさん
Dissolution of Diet

総選挙
そうせんきょ
General election

特別国会
とくべつこっかい
Special meeting of Diet

内閣総辞職
ないかくそう じ しょく
Resignation of Cabinet

総理大臣指名
そう り だいじん し めい
Appointment of Prime
Minister

総理大臣はそのまま
そう り だいじん
Prime Minister
remains in post.

改造内閣
かいぞうないかく
Cabinet reshuffling

新内閣
しんないかく
New Cabinet

皇居で天皇による認証式が行われ、組閣が完了
こうきょ　てんのう　　　　　　 にんしょうしき　おこな　　　そ かく　かんりょう

The formation of the Cabinet is completed when the attestation ceremony has been
held by the Emperor at the Imperial Palace.

□ 認証式　attestation ceremony
□ 組閣　formation of a cabinet

10

政治・司法

内閣は、**行政の最高府**である。その**職権**は「**内閣法**」が定めるところだが、内閣の長である総理大臣が招集する閣議によって職権が行使される。閣議は、週2回の**定例閣議**のほかに臨時閣議、**持ち回り閣議**があり、いずれも行政の最高の意思決定機関である。閣議は**国家機密**事項を討議するケースも多いため、秘密会になっていて、**全員一致**が原則である。ただし、閣議内容は、通常の場合には内閣官房長官を通じて公表される。

内閣には、衆議院の解散権、予算作成、法案の提出権、最高裁判所の長官の指名および判事の任命権、**条約の締結権**などがある。一方、内閣は衆議院が**不信任**を議決したときは、総辞職しなければならない。

□行政の最高府　the highest administrative branch of the government
□職権　authority
□内閣法　Cabinet law
□定例　regular
□閣議　Cabinet meeting

□持ち回り閣議　round-robin meeting
□国家機密　national secret
□全員一致　unanimous vote
□条約の締結　conclude treaty
□不信任　no confidence

The Cabinet

The Cabinet is the highest administrative branch of the government. It is formed and headed by the Prime Minister, while the Cabinet Law delineates its authority. The Cabinet meets twice weekly, although special and round-robin meetings may also be held. Whatever the form of its meeting, the Cabinet represents the highest decision-making government body. Because the Cabinet often discusses national secrets, the meetings are closed to the public and decisions are made by unanimous vote. Under normal circumstances, however, the contents of the discussions are made public through the chief Cabinet secretary.

The Cabinet has the right to dissolve the House of Representatives, prepare budgets, submit legislation, appoint the justices of the Supreme Court, and conclude treaties. However, if the House of Representatives reaches a decision of no confidence, then the entire Cabinet must resign.

政治・司法

行政の最高府
Highest body of government administration

内閣
Cabinet

全員集合！

The Cabinet will now meet!

総理
Prime Minister

内閣総理大臣（１名）と大臣（17名以内）で構成される
Composed of the Prime Minister (1) and Ministers (up to 17).

内閣府	Cabinet Office
内閣法制局	Cabinet Legislation Bureau
安全保障会議	Security Council
人事院	National Personnel Authority
会計検査院	Board of Audit

各省庁
Ministries and agencies

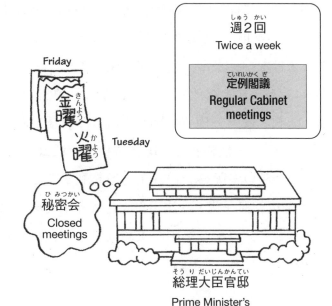

週2回
Twice a week

定例閣議
Regular Cabinet meetings

Friday

金曜

火曜
Tuesday

秘密会
Closed meetings

総理大臣官邸
Prime Minister's official residence

閣議
Cabinet meetings

全員一致が原則
Decisions by unanimous vote

一堂に会さず、決裁書を各大臣に回すことで行う
Ministers examine bills individually.

持ち回り閣議
Round-robin Cabinet meetings

必要に応じて随時開催
Cabinet meetings are held as occasion demands.

臨時閣議
Extraordinary Cabinet meetings

イギリスの内閣
The U.K. Cabinet

イギリスでは与党内閣とは別に、野党第一党による影の内閣（シャドー・キャビネット）が正式に認められていて、いつでも政権交代が可能なようにしてある

In the U.K., in addition to the Cabinet of the ruling party, there is also an officially approved Shadow Cabinet of the leading opposition party. As a result, authority can be transferred at any time.

□構成される composed of
□決裁書 approval document

□随時 at any time
□与党 ruling party

□野党第一党 leading opposition party

議員特権のしくみ

政治・司法

◁))　国会議員には、国民の代表として職務を遂行するための特権が与えられている。第1に「不逮捕特権」で、国会の会期中は現行犯以外は逮捕されることはない。また、会期前に逮捕された議員は、所属する議院の要求があれば会期中に釈放される。第2は「免責特権」で、国会内で行った発言・演説・投票の内容に関して院外で責任を問われることはない。第3が「歳費を受ける権利」で、国会議員は一般公務員の最高額の給料より少なくない金額の歳費（給与）をもらう権利があることに加えて、期末手当・調査研究広報滞在費・立法事務委託費等が支給される。また、議員が任命する秘書3名分の給与を国が支給するなど、待遇面でさまざまな配慮がされている。

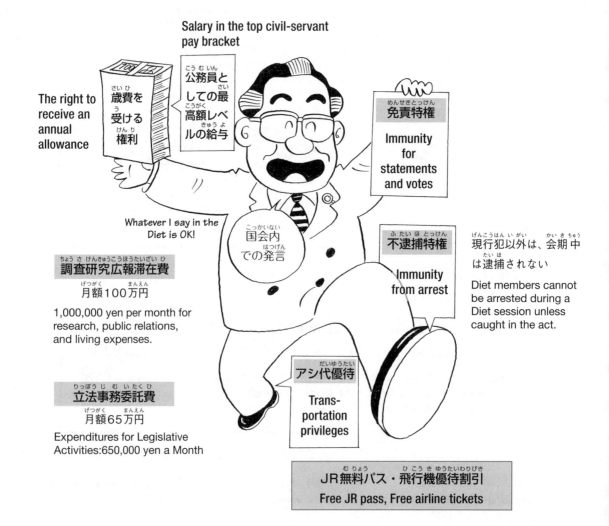

Diet Member Privileges

As representatives of the Japanese people, Diet members are granted special privileges to enable them to carry out their responsibilities. The first is immunity from arrest. During a Diet session, a Diet member cannot be arrested unless he or she is caught in the act of committing a crime. Members arrested before a Diet session can be freed for the period of the session at the demand of the House to which they belong. Second, Diet members are granted immunity for what they say and how they vote in the Diet, and they cannot be held responsible for any of those things outside the Diet. Third, Diet members receive a variety of compensations. They must be paid at least as much as the highest salary of regular civil servants. They also receive end-of-term allowances, research and public relations subsistence expenses, and legislative assistance allowances. The government also pays the salaries of three secretaries for each Diet member.

議員月額歳費 Monthly Salary for Diet Members:
129万7000円 1,297,000 yen

期末手当 Term-end allowance
年額約583万円（2回に分けて支給） Annual Amount: 5,830,000 yen (paid biannually)

議長月額 Monthly salary for President	218万2000円 2,182,000 yen
副議長月額 Monthly salary for Vice-President	159万3000円 1,593,000 yen

（2021年時点　As of 2021）

□遂行する carry out
□特権 privilege
□不逮捕特権 immunity from arrest
□現行犯 be caught in the act of committing a crime
□釈放される be freed
□免責特権 immunity for statements and votes

□歳費 compensation, salary
□一般公務員 regular civil servant
□期末手当 end-of-term allowance
□調査研究広報滞在費 research and public relations subsistence expenses
□立法事務委託費 legislative assistance allowance

政党のしくみ

政治・司法

◁))) 憲法21条に「結社の自由」が保障されてはいるものの、政党の定義は憲法や国会法にはない。ドイツのように「政党法」を設けている国もあるが、日本では政党を法律で規制すると活動の自由がおびやかされる、との意見が支配的。しかし、議会制民主主義では、政党の役割がきわめて重要であることはいうまでもない。ただ、国会法では2人以上の議員で結成できる「会派」が認められていて、実質的には、会派と政党はほぼイコールである。
　"政権を取らぬ政党はネズミを取らぬ猫のようなもの"という言葉が象徴するように、善悪は別にしてすべての政党は政権獲得に走るものだ。

◁))) 「公職選挙法」での政党とは、小選挙区は立候補議員5人以上か得票率2%以上、比例区は名簿登載数がブロック定数の2割以上とされる

Under the Public Offices Election Law, political parties are defined as groups that have five or more candidates or obtain 2% or more of the vote in single-seat constituencies, and in proportional districts have candidates representing 20% of the total number of district representatives.

政党交付金
Subsidies for political parties

◁))) 「政党助成法」に基づき、政党の活動費を国が補助することになった。所属国会議員数や国政選挙の得票率などで一定の要件を満たし、法人登記をした政党がこの交付金を受け取れる

Under the Party Subsidies Law, the national government provides financial support for political parties that satisfy certain conditions, such as the number of affiliated Diet members and the percentage of votes they receive in national elections. The parties also have to be registered corporations.

□結社の自由 freedom of association
□定義 definition
□支配的 dominant

□議会制民主主義 parliamentary democracy
□会派 parliamentary group
□象徴する symbolize

□公職選挙法 the Public Offices Election Law
□小選挙区 single-seat constituency
□比例区 proportional district

Political Parties

Article 21 of the Japanese Constitution guarantees freedom, association and assembly, but nothing in the Constitution or the Diet Law defines a political party. While some countries such as Germany have laws governing political parties, in Japan the dominant view is that such laws would threaten their freedom. However, political parties play a very important role in parliamentary democracy, and Japan's Diet Law even recognizes the formation of parliamentary groups of two or more members as essentially the same as a party.

There's a saying that "political parties that don't gain power are like cats that don't catch mice." For better or worse, all political parties try to form governments.

Politics and Legislation

Party A

○ ○ 党

各政党の前年収入総額（借入金、助成金、繰越金などを除いた実収入）を基準に交付される

Party subsidies are based on the respective party's annual net income (excluding borrowed money, subsidies, funds held over from previous years, etc.).

政党交付金

Political party subsidies

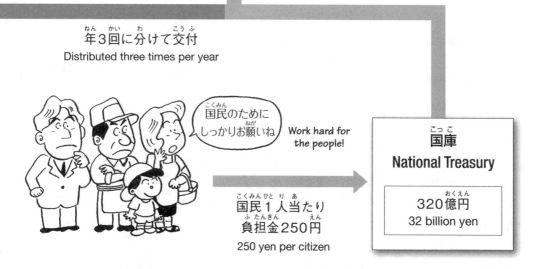

年3回に分けて交付

Distributed three times per year

国民のためにしっかりお願いね

Work hard for the people!

国民1人当たり負担金250円

250 yen per citizen

国庫
National Treasury

320億円

32 billion yen

□ 一定の要件 certain conditions
□ 法人登記 corporate registration
□ 繰越金 fund held over from previous years

政治・司法

正しい政治献金
Proper political contributions

企業・労働組合
Companies and labor unions

政党と、政党の**政治資金団体**に対する寄付に限り、企業の規模に応じて年間750万円以内から年間1億円以内までの範囲で可

Companies can contribute between 7.5 and 100 million yen per year to political parties and their fund-raising groups, depending on the size of the company.

Contributions to individual politicians are forbidden!

政治家個人に対する献金はダメー

コレハドウモ

コンゴトモヨロシク

民間企業
Private company

労働組合
Labor union

企業
Company

年間の**枠**を超えなければいくらでも**可**

Any amount is acceptable, as long as it does not exceed the annual maximum.

企業や労働組合などが**大口献金をする**場合は、政党・政党の政治資金団体だけに限られ、個人献金はできない

Companies, labor unions, and other large contributors can donate money only to political parties and their fund-raising groups. They cannot contribute to individual politicians.

The names of recipients must be made public.

献金先を公開しなければなりません

Company

(株)○○○

○○党
Party

一律
5万円超

Over 50,000 yen per party

個人
Individuals

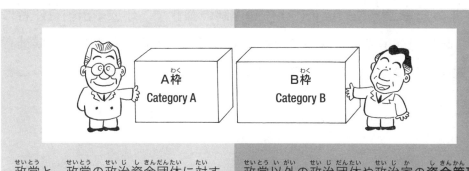

| A枠
Category A | B枠
Category B |

政党と、政党の政治資金団体に対する寄付（年間2000万円まで）

Contributions to political parties and to political funding groups for political parties (up to 20 million yen per year)

政党以外の政治団体や政治家の資金管理団体に対する寄付（年間1000万円まで）

Contributions to political organizations other than political parties and to fund-managing organizations for politicians (up to 10 million yen per year)

年間2000万円以内ならいくらでも可

Any amount up to 20 million yen per year is okay.

年間150万円以内

No more than 1.5 million yen per year

年間150万円以内

No more than 1.5 million yen per year

年間150万円以内

No more than 1.5 million yen per year

政治家
Politicians

政治資金団体
Fund-raising groups

政党
Political party

資金管理団体
fund-managing organizations

1団体のみ　One group only

政治団体
Political party

政治団体
Political party

□政治資金団体　political fund-raising group

□年間の枠　annual maximum

□献金をする　donate money

□資金管理団体　fund-managing organization

13

立候補のしくみ

政治・司法

選挙に対する国民の関心は年々薄れてゆく一方で、国政選挙の投票率は下降気味である。戦いすんで日が暮れて、あとに残された関心事は選挙違反報道という情けなさも相変わらずだ。

94年の公職選挙法の改正による連座制の強化で、親族や出納責任者に加えて秘書が選挙違反を犯して禁固以上の刑に処せられた場合にも候補者の当選は無効になり、さらに5年間は同じ選挙区から立候補できないことになった。

□関心 interest
□年々 year by year
□投票率 voter turnout
□選挙違反 election law violation
□公職選挙法 Public Offices Election law

□連座制 the punishment of people associated with violations of the law
□出納責任者 treasurer
□禁固 imprisonment

Running for Office

The public interest in elections has been dropping steadily, and voter turnout for national elections is on the decline. And once an election is over, the only thing left of interest is news about election law violations.

In 1994, when the Public Offices Election Law was revised to toughen the punishment of people associated with violations of the law, politicians' secretaries came to be subject to imprisonment for violating elections laws, not only their relatives and treasurers. Election results may also be declared null and void due to violations, and candidates prohibited from running for office from the same district for the next five years.

年齢条件さえ満たしていれば誰でも立候補できるが、国政選挙には供託金制度がある

Anyone can run for office as long as they meet the age conditions. For national elections, though, candidates must also put up deposits.

Candidate A

届け出　Application

供託金 Deposits

国政選挙では個人立候補者は300万円、政党の立候補者は300万円、600万円。泡沫候補やミニ政党の乱立を防止するのが目的で原則として全額返還されるが、所定の得票数に達しない場合には国庫に没収される

In the 2005 House of Representatives election, candidates had to submit deposits of 3 million yen each for proportionally represented seats. For single-seat constituencies, candidates had to deposit 3 million yen if running for single seats and twice that amount if running for multiple seats. The purpose of the deposits is to prevent frivolous candidacies and the proliferation of tiny political parties. The deposits are generally returned to the candidates, but they are confiscated for the national treasury if the candidates do not obtain a minimum number of votes.

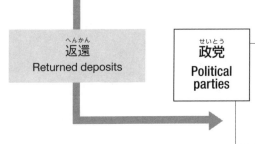

返還
Returned deposits

政党
Political parties

政党の場合は当選者数の2倍の金額

For political parties, the amount returned is twice that paid for the number of elected candidates.

□供託金　deposit
□泡沫候補　fringe candidate

□乱立　proliferation
□没収する　confiscate

◁))

国政選挙での選挙運動期間は衆院選が12日間、参院選が17日間である

The campaign period during national elections is 12 days for the House of Representatives and 17 days for the House of Councillors.

選挙管理委員会

Election Administration Commission

◁)) 立候補者に認められる法定選挙費用の上限は、選挙の種類により異なる。国政選挙の場合は、2500万円〜5200万円

Legal maximum funding for candidates in political elections depends on the type of election. For national elections, it ranges from 25 million yen to 52 million yen.

事前ポスター
Advance posters

Reporting committee for Candidate A

◁))

立候補予定者の顔を大写しにした政治活動用の事前ポスターは、任期が満了する6か月前からは貼り出してはならないことになっている

Advance posters show large photographs of potential candidates and are used for their political activities. However, they cannot be displayed within six months of the end of a politician's term of office.

14

政治（せいじ）・司法（しほう）

◁))　日本（にほん）の裁判（さいばん）は同（おな）じ事件（じけん）について、3回（かい）まで裁判（さいばん）を求（もと）めることができる三審制（さんしんせい）をとっている。まず第一審（だいいっしん）では、ごく軽（かる）い事件（じけん）は**簡易裁判所（かんいさいばんしょ）**、家庭問題（かていもんだい）や未成年者（みせいねんしゃ）の事件（じけん）は**家庭裁判所（かていさいばんしょ）**、それ以外（いがい）の事件（じけん）は**地方裁判所（ちほうさいばんしょ）**で行（おこな）われる。第一審判決（だいいっしんはんけつ）に不服（ふふく）の場合（ばあい）、裁判（さいばん）のやり直（なお）し（第二審（だいにしん））を求（もと）めることを**控訴（こうそ）**という。第二審判決（だいにしんはんけつ）にも不服（ふふく）の場合（ばあい）、**上告（じょうこく）**によって第三審（だいさんしん）を求（もと）めることができる。また、下級裁判所（かきゅうさいばんしょ）の決定（けってい）・命令（めいれい）について上級裁判所（じょうきゅうさいばんしょ）へ不服（ふふく）を申（もう）し立（た）てる場合（ばあい）、控訴（こうそ）や上告（じょうこく）よりも簡単（かんたん）でスピーディーな方法（ほうほう）として、抗告（こうこく）がある。

□三審制　three hearings

□簡易裁判所　summary court

□家庭裁判所　family court

□地方裁判所　district court

□判決　verdict

□控訴　appeal

□上告　final appeal

Trials

Trials in Japan allow up to three hearings per case. The first hearing for minor cases is held at a summary court; family matters and cases involving minors are handled by family courts. The first hearings for other cases take place at the district courts. If either side disagrees with the verdict of the first hearing, they can appeal for a second hearing; this is called a *kōso* appeal. If they are still dissatisfied with that result, they can submit an appeal for a third hearing; this is called a *jōkoku* appeal. A third type of appeal, called a *kōkoku* appeal, offers a simpler and faster way (compared with *kōso* and *jōkoku* appeals) for appealing lower court verdicts and orders to higher courts.

政治・司法
せいじ・しほう

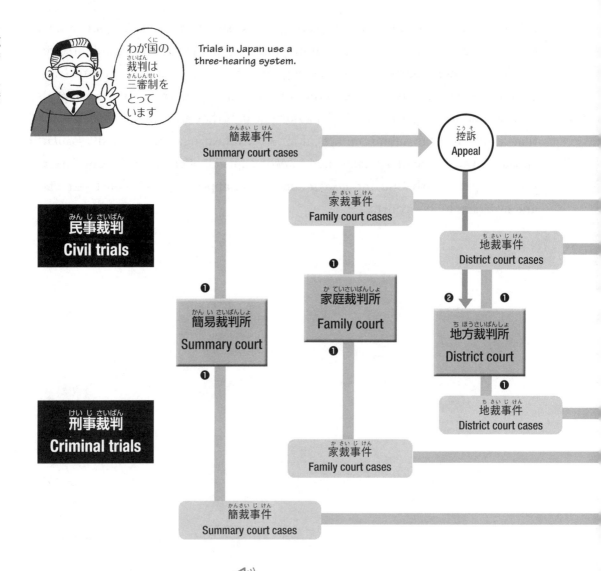

わが国の裁判は三審制をとっています

Trials in Japan use a three-hearing system.

簡裁事件
Summary court cases

控訴
Appeal

家裁事件
Family court cases

地裁事件
District court cases

民事裁判
Civil trials

簡易裁判所
Summary court

家庭裁判所
Family court

地方裁判所
District court

地裁事件
District court cases

刑事裁判
Criminal trials

家裁事件
Family court cases

簡裁事件
Summary court cases

Conciliation committee　調停委員

Judge　裁判官

簡易裁判所には、話し合いで解決させる**民事調停制度**や、60万円以下の金銭請求事件を原則として1回で審理して判決を下す**少額訴訟制度**がある

Summary courts handle civil cases that can be resolved through discussions. They also conduct one-hearing trials for small-claims cases for amounts under 600,000 yen.

□民事調停制度　Civil Mediation System　　　　□少額訴訟制度　Small Claims Litigation System

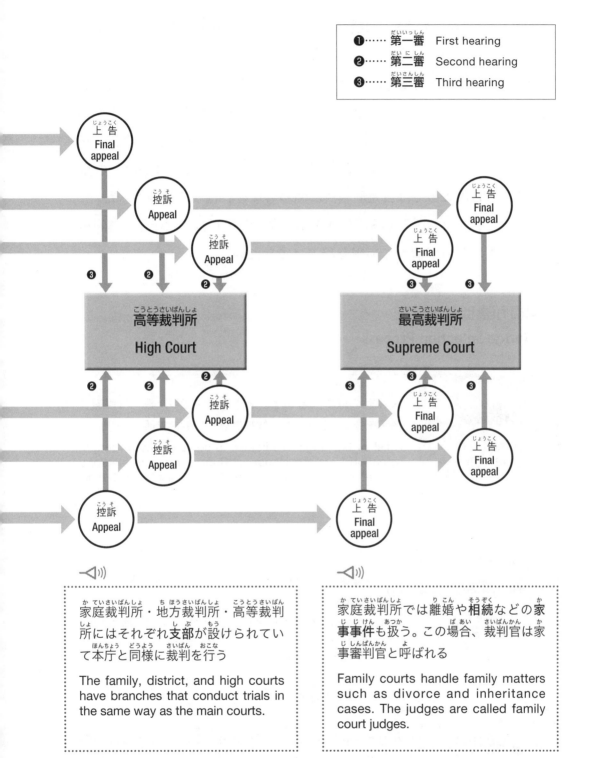

❶······ 第一審 First hearing
❷······ 第二審 Second hearing
❸······ 第三審 Third hearing

上告
Final appeal

控訴
Appeal

控訴
Appeal

上告
Final appeal

上告
Final appeal

高等裁判所
High Court

最高裁判所
Supreme Court

控訴
Appeal

控訴
Appeal

控訴
Appeal

上告
Final appeal

上告
Final appeal

控訴
Appeal

上告
Final appeal

◁))

家庭裁判所・地方裁判所・高等裁判所にはそれぞれ支部が設けられていて本庁と同様に裁判を行う

The family, district, and high courts have branches that conduct trials in the same way as the main courts.

◁))

家庭裁判所では離婚や相続などの家事事件も扱う。この場合、裁判官は家事審判官と呼ばれる

Family courts handle family matters such as divorce and inheritance cases. The judges are called family court judges.

□支部 branch   □相続 inheritance   □家事事件 family matter

73

裁判員制度のしくみ

15

◁))) 　2009年5月から始まった**裁判員制度**は、国民が裁判員として**刑事裁判**に参加し、裁判官との**評議**によって**被告人**の有罪・無罪、**量刑**を決める新制度である。従来の刑事裁判は、法律の専門家を中心に運営されてきたため、国民にわかりにくく、しかも**審理**に極めて長期間かかるという難点があった。それを改善するための制度とはいえ、殺人事件などの重大事件の第1審が対象とされるのは、一般国民にとって裁判員になるのはかなりの重圧になる。場合によっては、死刑判決に関わらなければならないからだ。

　選挙権がある日本国民（18歳以上）なら誰もが裁判員に選任される可能性があり、よほどの事情がない限り辞退はできない。

◁))) ## 裁判員が選ばれるまで
Lay Judge Selection Process

候補者選定 Selection of Candidates	衆議院の選挙人名簿から無作為に抽出した裁判員候補者名簿を作成。事件ごとに候補者をくじ引きで選ぶ A list of lay judge candidates is compiled by a random selection from the House of Representatives electoral register. Lay judges are chosen from this list for each trial.

質問票送付 Mailing of Questionnaires	事件の審理が始まる6か月前までに候補者に通知をする。原則として辞退できない Candidates are notified six months before the beginning of the trial. As a rule, candidates cannot decline.

裁判員選任 Selection of Lay Judges	裁判所が指定した期日に選任され、事件内容についての守秘義務が課せられる Lay judges are selected on a day set by the court and are sworn to secrecy concerning the nature of the trial.

Lay Judge System

In May 2009 a new system was implemented whereby citizens acting as lay judges in criminal trials confer with judges to determine whether defendants are guilty or innocent as well as the nature of their punishment. In traditional criminal trials carried out by legal specialists, ordinary citizens found them difficult to follow, and the trials themselves tended to drag out for excessive lengths of time. Even though this system is seen as a means of rectifying these drawbacks, since it concerns the initial trial of serious crimes such as murder, the possibility of becoming a lay judge puts a great of pressure on ordinary citizens. Depending on the case, they may have to take part in a death sentence.

For any Japanese citizen with the right to vote (18 or over), there is the possibility of being selected as a lay judge. Except for the most pressing cases, there is no possibility of being excused from this duty.

刑事裁判の法廷
Criminal Trial Courtroom

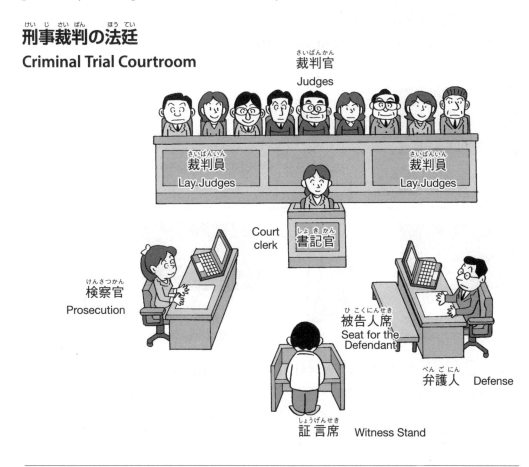

裁判官
Judges

裁判員
Lay Judges

裁判員
Lay Judges

Court clerk 書記官

検察官
Prosecution

被告人席
Seat for the Defendant

弁護人　Defense

証言席　Witness Stand

- □ 裁判員制度　lay judge system
- □ 刑事裁判　criminal trial
- □ 評議　confer with
- □ 被告人　defendant
- □ 量刑　assessment of case
- □ 審理　trial
- □ 重圧　great of pressure
- □ 無作為　random
- □ 抽出　selection
- □ 守秘　secrecy

16

判決のしくみ

◁)) 日本の裁判所は、最高裁判所、**高等裁判所**、地方裁判所、家庭裁判所、簡易裁判所からなる。最高裁判所以外の4つの裁判所を**下級裁判所**という。

最高裁判所は、長官と14名の裁判官で構成され、長官は内閣の指名にもとづき天皇が任命し、他の裁判官は内閣が任命する。下級裁判所の裁判官は、最高裁判所が指名する名簿から内閣が任命する。

最高裁判所の裁判官の人選基準は、裁判官出身が6名、弁護士出身が4名、検察官及び官庁出身が各2名、法学者1名とされている。40歳以上、70歳が定年で10年ごとに**国民審査**がある。

下級裁判所の判決のしくみ
How lower courts reach their verdicts

簡易裁判所
Summary courts

1名の裁判官による単独制
Verdicts are reached by only one judge.

全国に438か所
438 courts nationwide

家庭裁判所
Family courts

全国に50か所
50 courts nationwide

1名の裁判官による単独制が原則だが、重要事件は3名の**合議制**

In general, verdicts are reached by only one judge, but important cases are decided by a council of three judges.

地方裁判所
District courts

全国に50か所
50 courts nationwide

1名の裁判官による単独制が原則だが、合議制をとるケースもある

In general, verdicts are reached by only one judge, but sometimes a council of judges renders the verdict.

☐ 高等裁判所 high court ☐ 基準 criteria ☐ 合議制 council system
☐ 下級裁判所 lower court ☐ 国民審査 national review

Verdicts

The Japanese court system consists of the Supreme Court, high courts, district courts, family courts, and summary courts, with these four types of courts under the Supreme Court referred to collectively as lower courts. The Supreme Court consists of the Chief Justice and 14 justices. The Chief Justice is chosen by the Cabinet and appointed by the Emperor, while the other justices are appointed by the Cabinet. The judges in the lower courts are appointed by the Cabinet based on a list of names prepared by the Supreme Court.

The criteria for the selection of judges of the Supreme Court are six from thejudiciary, four from the bar, two each from prosecutors and government offices, and one legal scholar. The minimum age is 40, and the mandatory retirement age is 70. The justices are subject to popular review every 10 years.

こうとうさいばんしょ
高等裁判所
High courts

ぜんこく　　　　しょ
全国に8か所
8 courts nationwide

めい　　さいばんかん　　　ごうぎ
3名の裁判官による合議
せい　げんそく
制が原則

Verdicts are reached by three judges.

か きゅうさいばんしょ　　はんけつ　　と　　け　　　　へんこう　　もと　　　　　　　　　　　こうそ　　じょうこく　　　　　　さいばんしょ
下級裁判所の判決の取り消し・変更を求めることを控訴・上告といい、裁判所
けってい　めいれい　たい　　　ふ ふく　うった　　　こうこく　とくべつこうこく
の決定・命令に対する不服の訴えを抗告・特別抗告という

Asking for the repeal or change of a lower court's decision is called an intermediate or final appeal; registering a complaint against a court decision or order is called a complaint or a special complaint.

かん い さいばんしょ　か ていさいばんしょ　ち ほうさいばんしょ　　　さいばん　そ しょう い がい　とう じ しゃどう し　　はな　あ
簡易裁判所、家庭裁判所、地方裁判所には裁判（訴訟）以外に当事者同士の話し合いによる
かいけつ　めざ　　ちょうてい い いんかい　　もう　　　　　　　　　ちょうてい い いん　べん ご し　ゆうしきしゃ　　　　　えら
解決を目指す「調停委員会」が設けられている。調停委員は弁護士や有識者などから選ば
ちゅうりつてき　たち ば　わ かい
れ、中立的な立場で和解をすすめる

In addition to court proceedings (lawsuits), Summary Courts, Family Courts, and District Courts have "arbitration committees" that aim to resolve disputes through discussion between the parties. Mediators are selected from attorneys, experts, and others to promote settlement from a neutral perspective.

□調停委員会 arbitration committee　　　　□調停委員 mediator　　　　□中立的 neutral

政治・司法

最高裁判所の判決のしくみ
How the Supreme Court works

◁))

最高裁判所の裁判部門は、**大法廷**と３つの**小法廷**からなる。長官を含め裁判官は15名しかいないため、審理の**補佐役**として最高裁判所調査官が配置されている。下級裁判所の調査官は一般職員だが、最高裁判所に限り裁判官から任命され、裁判官のエリートコースとされる

The judicial framework of the Supreme Court is composed of the Grand Bench and three Petty Benches. Since there are only fifteen justices on the Court, including the Chief Justice, judicial research officials are assigned to act as assistants during proceedings. Such officials in the lower courts are ordinary civil servants, but those working specifically for the Supreme Court are appointed by a Supreme Court Justice. This is considered the fast track to becoming a justice.

小法廷
Petty Bench

5名の裁判官による合議制
Council of five justices

◁))

小法廷で審理した事件の中で処分が憲法に適合しているかどうか判断する必要がある場合に限り、大法廷で裁判を行う

When a case before a Petty Bench requires a decision concerning constitutionality, the case is tried and judged by the Grand Bench.

□ 大法廷　Grand Bench
□ 小法廷　Petty Bench
□ 補佐役　assistant
□ 調査官　research official
□ 検察　prosecution
□ 証人　witness

🔊

_{した}　_{ほうていず}　_{けいじじけん}　_{ばあい}　_{みんじじけん}　_{ばあい}　_{べんごにんせき}　_{じょうこくにんがわせき}　_{けんさつ}
下の法廷図は刑事事件の場合で、民事事件の場合には弁護人席が上告人側席、検察
_{かんせき}　_{ひ じょうこくにんがわせき}
官席が被上告人側席となる

The diagram below shows the court layout for a criminal case. In a civil case, the seats for the defense are replaced by the seats for the plaintiff, and the prosecution's seats are taken by the defendant.

大法廷　_{だいほうてい}
Grand Bench

_{めい}　_{ぜんさいばんかん}
15名の全裁判官による
_{ごうぎせい}
合議制

Council of all 15 justices

_{さいばんしょ}　_{ぜんいん}　_{いけん}　_{ひょうじ}　_{はんけつ}　_{た すうけつ}
裁判書には全員の意見を表示し、判決は多数決による
_{さいこうさいばんしょ}　_{はんけつ}　_{とくちょう}
のが最高裁判所の判決の特 徴

The written verdict includes the judgments of all of the justices. In the Supreme Court, verdicts are reached by majority vote.

_{さいばんちょう}　_{ちょうかん}
裁判長（長官）Chief Justice

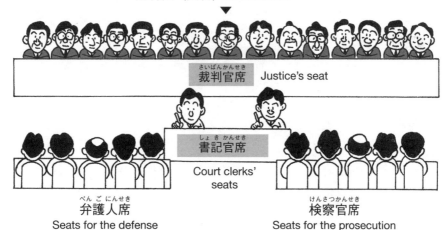

_{さいばんかんせき}
裁判官席　Justice's seat

_{しょ き かんせき}
書記官席
Court clerks' seats

_{べん ご にんせき}
弁護人席
Seats for the defense

_{けんさつかんせき}
検察官席
Seats for the prosecution

_{さいこうさいばんしょ}　_{ほうてい}　_{しょうにんせき}
最高裁判所の法廷には証人席はない
There is no witness box in the Supreme Court courtroom.

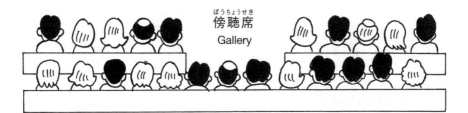

_{ぼうちょうせき}
傍聴席
Gallery

17

1989年、国連は「死刑廃止条約」を採択したが、日本はこの条約を批准していない死刑存置国である。国連加盟国で死刑制度を撤廃したり、制度が残っていても刑を停止している国は50余り。ヨーロッパや中南米に多く、先進国で死刑制度を採用しているのは日本とアメリカ合衆国ぐらいということから、死刑廃止論議も巻き起こっている。裁判によって死刑が確定すると、6か月以内に**法務大臣**が**執行命令**を下さねばならないが、命令書へのサインを拒む大臣もいる。

□存置 retain
□法務大臣 the Minister of Justice
□執行命令 order of execution

Death Penalty

In 1989, the United Nations General Assembly adopted a protocol aimed at eliminating the death penalty. Japan has not ratified that protocol and continues to impose capital punishment. Some 50 U.N. members, mostly in Europe and Latin America, have either abolished the death penalty or stopped implementing it. With Japan and the United States the only two major industrialized countries still executing convicted criminals, the abolition of the death penalty remains a topic of fervent debate in Japan. Within six months after a person has been sentenced to death by a court, the Minister of Justice must issue an order of execution, but some ministers refuse to sign the order.

Politics and Legislation

政治・司法

| 裁判所 Court | → 判決 Verdict → | 死刑確定 Death sentence |

判決謄本
公判記録
Official copy of verdict Court transcript

送付
Referral

検察庁
Public Prosecutor's Office

死刑が確定しても、死刑囚には執行までの間に、**再審請求や恩赦出願**のチャンスがある

Even after being sentenced to die, the prisoner has a chance to request a retrial or pardon before the sentence is carried out.

上申書
Written statement

提出
Submittal

法務省
Ministry of Justice

起案書作成
Execution proposal prepared

刑事局付の検事が判決を審査したうえで「死刑執行起案書」を書く

Prosecutors from the Criminal Affairs Bureau examine the verdict and prepare the execution proposal.

▼

「起案書」は、三局と官房の13人の幹部が**精読**したうえで大臣室に届けられる

The execution proposal is carefully read by thirteen senior officers from three Ministry of Justice bureaus and the Minister's secretariat and then delivered to the Minister's office.

執行命令
Execution order

「死刑事件審査結果」に法務大臣がサインし、その後「執行命令書」に公印が押される

When the Minister of Justice signs the "results of inquiry into a capital case," it is subsequently affixed with the official seal to become the order of execution.

Ummm...

う～ん

法務大臣

Minister of Justice

死刑執行の刑場があるのは東京、大阪、名古屋の3拘置所と福岡、札幌、仙台の3拘置支所である

Execution sites are located at three detention houses in Tokyo, Osaka, and Nagoya and at three prisons in Fukuoka, Sapporo, and Sendai.

執行
Execution

命令が出されてから5日以内に執行される

The convict is executed within five days after the order is issued.

□ 謄本　official copy
□ 再審　retrial
□ 恩赦出願　pardon
□ 刑事局　Criminal Affairs Bureau

□ 精読　carefully read
□ 公印　official seal
□ 拘置所　detention house

法曹界のしくみ

18

政治・司法

　法曹界は、裁判官、検察官、弁護士の3種類の**司法専門家**によって構成されている。これらの司法専門家になるには、国家試験である**司法試験**をパスすることが原則である。**司法修習生**になると、**実務研修**等を通じてそれぞれのコースを選択することになる。裁判官と検察官は公務員であり、弁護士は**独立開業**のコースだ。検察官のなかには、定年前に**退官**して弁護士になる人もいる。これを俗にヤメ検と称している。

　1993年から、弁護士の希望者のなかから裁判官や検察官に任官する制度が本格化したが、**待遇面での格差**をどう解消するかなどの難問を抱えている。また、検察官の任官では、優秀な**特捜事務官**を採用する制度もある。

□法曹界　the legal world
□司法専門家　legal expert
□司法試験　national bar examination
□司法修習生　legal apprentice
□実務研修　on-the-job training

□独立開業　operate independently
□退官する　retire
□待遇面での格差　salary gap
□特捜事務官　top public investigator

The Legal World

The legal world in Japan consists of three types of legal experts: judges, prosecutors, and lawyers. All must pass the national bar examination. When people have passed that exam and become legal apprentices, they receive on-the-job training and choose their career course. Judges or prosecutors are civil servants, while lawyers operate independently. Some prosecutors become lawyers after they retire; they are called *yameken*, or "prosecutors who have quit."

A new system was adopted in 1993 for appointing judges and prosecutors from among lawyers who wish such appointments, but difficulties remain, including the salary gap between the civil servants and private lawyers. There's also a procedure for appointing top public investigators as prosecutors.

政治・司法

司法試験
Bar exam

合格
Pass

2012年から受験資格は**法科大学院**修了者または**予備試験**合格者に限られ、5年間に3回の範囲内で受験できることになった。2021年の合格者は1421名（合格率42%）

From 2012, graduates of law schools and successful examinees of the preliminary exam will be allowed to take the exam for as many as three times within a period of five years. 1,421 examinees passed the test in 2021 (a success rate of 42%).

司法修習生
Legal apprenticeships

司法試験合格者が司法専門家になるには**司法修習所**に入らなければならない。修習期間は1年で、「2回試験」と呼ばれる試験を経てそれぞれ裁判官、検察官、弁護士の道へ進む

Those who pass the bar exam must complete an apprenticeship at a legal training center to become legal specialists. The training period is 12 months. During this time, apprentices must pass a test known as the "two-time exam" before they can go on to become judges, prosecutors, or lawyers.

□法科大学院　law school
□予備試験　preliminary exam
□司法修習所　legal training center
□顧客開拓する　develop a customer base

弁護士として独立開業するまでは、法律事務所に入って4
～5年実務をし、その間に**顧客開拓**もしておく

Before setting up their own legal practices, lawyers work
in law offices for four or five years, during which time they
develop a customer base.

弁護士が検察官や裁判官になるには、
経験年数、勤務年数の基準がある

To become judges or prosecutors, lawyers must have a certain number of years
of experience.

実務を4～5年
Four or five years
of work

弁護士
Lawyer

法律事務所
Law office

検察官
Prosecutor

採用試験
**Employment
test**

裁判官
Judge

裁判官、検察官は5年以上経験があればよい

Judges and prosecutors with five or more years of experience can
become lawyers.

検察庁のしくみ

19

政治・司法

　検察官が行う事務を統括する機関が検察庁である。検察庁は、裁判所の組織に対応する形で配置されている。検察官としては検事総長が最高位だが、指揮権は法務大臣がもつ。ただし、法務大臣は国会議員が就任することが通例であり、検察権の行使や司法の運営に政治的圧力が及ぶのを防ぐため、法務大臣は検事総長のみを指揮することができるという制限（検察庁法14条）がついている。この法務大臣の検事総長に対する指揮権は、1954年の「造船疑獄」で発動されたことがある。

　なお、東京・大阪・名古屋の3地方検察庁には、特別捜査部が設けられていて、いわゆる政治家がらみの事件などに対して、検察官中心の独自の捜査を行う。

□統括する　supervise
□裁判所の組織に対応する形で　in parallel to the court office

□検事総長　the Public Prosecutor General
□造船疑獄　shipbuilding bribery scandal
□特別捜査部　special investigation section

Public Prosecutor's Office

The work of public prosecutors is supervised by the Public Prosecutor's Office. This office is organized in parallel to the court system. The top prosecutor is the Public Prosecutor General, but the final authority over the office rests with the Minister of Justice. Because that minister is usually a member of the Diet, Article 14 of the Public Prosecutor's Office Law limits the minister's actual authority to the supervision of the Public Prosecutor General himself. The purpose of this restriction is to prevent political influence over prosecutions and legal procedures. This authority of the Minister of Justice over the Public Prosecutor General was exercised in 1954 to halt investigations into a shipbuilding bribery scandal.

The three district Public Prosecutor's Offices in Tokyo, Osaka, and Nagoya have special investigation sections that conduct independent investigations of political scandals and other sensitive cases.

Politics and Legislation

政治・司法

法務省
Ministry of Justice

検察に対して法務大臣は検事総長のみを指揮できる

The Minister of Justice has authority only over the Public Prosecutor General.

Authority

法務大臣

Minister of Justice

検事総長 Public Prosecutor General	最高検察庁（東京） Supreme Public Prosecutor's Office (Tokyo)
検事長 Superintendent Public Prosecutor	高等検察庁（8か所） High Public Prosecutor's Office (8 locations)
検事正 Chief Public Prosecutor	地方検察庁 District Public Prosecutor's Office
	区検察庁 Sub-District Prosecutor's Office

不起訴
No indictment

検察審査会
Committee for the Inquest of Prosecution

裁判所との関係
Relation to courts

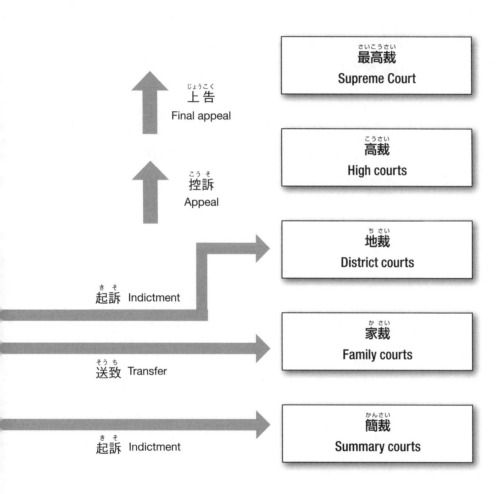

上告
Final appeal

控訴
Appeal

最高裁
Supreme Court

高裁
High courts

地裁
District courts

起訴 Indictment

家裁
Family courts

送致 Transfer

簡裁
Summary courts

起訴 Indictment

◁))

検察の**不起訴処分**の正当性を審査する機関。**地裁管内**から**クジ引き**で選ばれた11人の審査員で構成され、その議決には効力が与えられている

The committee, comprising 11 judges selected by lot from among members of district courts, studies whether decisions not to indict are justified. Its findings are referred back to the Prosecutor's Office and cases may be reopened.

□不起訴処分 decision not to indict   □クジ引き lot
□地裁管内 district court jurisdiction

20

警察庁のしくみ

政治・司法

◁)) 警察庁は、全国の警察の**総元締**である。警察庁が**管掌**する**管区**は全国に7管区あるが、東京の警視庁と北海道警察は長官直属の**別格扱い**となっている。長官をはじめとする警察庁の幹部の任免権は**国家公安委員会**にある。その長である**委員長**は国務大臣に相当し、国会議員が就任する。さらに、総理大臣は**長官**人事の承認および緊急時には警察を**統制する**ことができるため、いざというときの警察権の行使の限界がしばしば取り沙汰されてきた。

警察庁には、科学捜査などのための研究機関である**科学警察研究所**、幹部を養成するための警察大学校、皇居の警護や皇族を守ることを主務とする**皇宮警察本部**といった機関がある。

□ 総元締　governing body
□ 管掌　be in charge of
□ 管区　regional district
□ 別格扱いとなっている　be handled separately
□ 国家公安委員会　National Public Safety Commission

□ 委員長　Commissioner
□ 警察庁長官　NPA's Director-General
□ 統制する　take control of
□ 科学警察研究所　National Research Institute of Police Science
□ 皇宮警察本部　Imperial Guard Headquarters

National Police Agency

The National Police Agency (NPA) is in charge of the police throughout Japan, with operations divided into seven regional districts. However, the Metropolitan Police Department in Tokyo and the Hokkaido Police are handled separately under the direct control of the Director-General of the NPA. The Director-General and other senior officers of the NPA are appointed by the National Public Safety Commisssion, the Commissioner of which is a member of the Diet and ranks as a minister of state. The Prime Minister approves the appointment of the Director-General and can take control of the police during emergencies, an arrangement that often raises questions about the limits on police powers in extreme situations.

Under the NPA are the National Research Institute of Police Science, which studies scientific investigation methods; the National Police Academy, where senior officers are trained; and the Imperial Guard Headquarters, which guards the Imperial Palace and protects the Imperial Family.

政治・司法

国家公安委員会
National Public Safety Commission

委員長（国務大臣）と5名の委員で構成する警察幹部の任免権をもった最高機関

This commission, which consists of a Commissioner (a minister of state) and five other members, is the highest body supervising the police. It appoints senior police officers.

国務大臣
Minister of State

警察庁長官
Director-General of the NPA

内閣総理大臣
Prime Minister

長官人事を承認するほか、緊急時には警察を統制する

The Prime Minister approves the appointment of the NPA's Director-General and can take control of the police during emergencies.

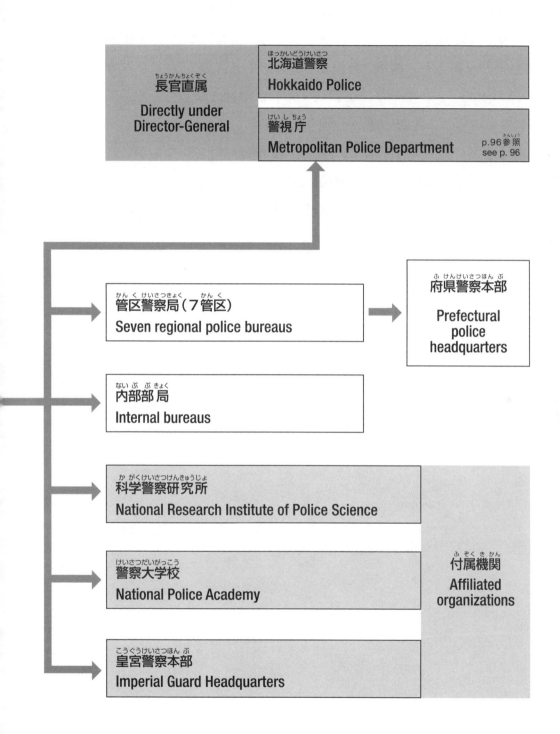

長官直属
Directly under Director-General

ほっかいどうけいさつ
北海道警察
Hokkaido Police

けいしちょう
警視庁
Metropolitan Police Department

さんしょう
p.96参照
see p. 96

かんくけいさつきょく　かんく
管区警察局（7管区）
Seven regional police bureaus

ふけんけいさつほんぶ
府県警察本部
Prefectural police headquarters

ないぶぶきょく
内部部局
Internal bureaus

かがくけいさつけんきゅうじょ
科学警察研究所
National Research Institute of Police Science

けいさつだいがっこう
警察大学校
National Police Academy

こうぐうけいさつほんぶ
皇宮警察本部
Imperial Guard Headquarters

ふぞくきかん
付属機関
Affiliated organizations

政治・司法

テレビドラマで活躍している**刑事**は、東京・桜田門の警視庁**刑事部**に所属する警察官である。刑事部の各課の中でも、捜査一課は東京都内で起きた凶悪犯罪を担当し、**課長（警視正）**はキャリア官僚が大半を占める警視庁幹部の中で、ノンキャリアが就任するのが慣例となっている。ドラマの舞台になるのもこの捜査一課が圧倒的に多い。

刑事は通常の捜査では私服であり、**階級章**はつけていないが、一般の警察官と同様の階級がある。この階級を上げるためには昇級試験を受けなければならない。だが、昇級せずに生涯**ヒラ刑事で通す**のが刑事**魂**だという**気風**も、ドラマ同様にあるようだ。

□刑事 police detective
□刑事部 Criminal Investigation Bureau
□課長 section chief
□警視正 chief superintendent

□階級章 rank marking
□ヒラ刑事で通す stay at the lowest rank
□気風 ethos

Metropolitan Police Department

The police detectives depicted in television dramas are usually police officers attached to the Criminal Investigation Bureau of the Metropolitan Police Department in Sakuradamon, Tokyo. This bureau is divided into several sections, with the first investigation section considered most prestigious. It handles violent crimes committed in the Tokyo metropolitan area. A particularly elite position is chief superintendent. The majority of the Metropolitan Police Department's managing staff are career civil servants, but it has become commonplace for non-career civil servants to accept positions there as well. Many dramas take place in this section.

During normal investigations, the detectives wear street clothes without rank markings even though their rank is the same as that of regular police officers. They must pass promotion tests if they want to rise in rank. As in the TV dramas, many of the detectives feel that, to be true detectives, they should stay at the lowest rank for their entire careers.

政治・司法

警視総監
Director of MPD

警視監
Superintendent
general

警視長
Superintendent
supervisor

国家公安委員会 National Public Safety Commission
警察庁長官 Director-General, National Police Agency
東京都公安委員会 Tokyo Public Safety Commission

統制　Supervision

警視庁　Metropolitan Police Department

方面本部(8方面) Eight district headquarters	警察署 Police stations

署長　Police chief

警視正から上の階級に昇進できるのは少数のエリートだけ

Only a few elite personnel can rise in rank above chief superintendent.

警視正
Chief
superintendent

警視
Superintendent

警部
Inspector

警察署長は警視が一般的で、大警察署の場合は警視正がなる。警視（正）は警視庁では課長クラスで、第一線の指揮官の立場

Most police stations are headed by superintendents, with only the larger stations headed by chief superintendents. Superintendents and chief superintendents are the equivalent of section chiefs in the Metropolitan Police Department hierarchy. They supervise operations on the front lines.

◁))

警視庁のトップは警視総監だが、この階級は警察官としては最高位で、任命権は総理大臣がもつ

The head of the Metropolitan Police Department is the highest ranking police officer. He is appointed by the Prime Minister.

交番
Police boxes
複数の警察官が交代勤務
Several police officers work rotating shifts.

駐在所
Residential police boxes
1名の警察官が家族と同居して勤務
One officer lives at the police box with his or her family.

警察官の階級　Police officer ranks

警部補	巡査部長	巡査長	巡査
Assistant inspector	Police sergeant	Head patrol officer	Patrol officer

◁))

警部補以上は司法警察員、巡査部長以下は司法巡査とも呼ばれる。巡査長は正式な階級ではない

Assistant police inspectors and below are judicial police officers, and police sergeants and below are referred to as judicial police constables. The title master patrol officer is not an official rank.

Chapter 2
Executive Branch

<ruby>第<rt></rt></ruby>2<ruby>章<rt>だいにしょう</rt></ruby> <ruby>行<rt>ぎょう</rt></ruby> <ruby>政<rt>せい</rt></ruby>

知らなかったことがすっきりわかる！
Clearing away the Cobwebs

22

中央省庁のしくみ

◁)) 　国会で決まった法律や予算にもとづいて政治を行うのが政府で、それを分野別に担当しているのが**中央官庁**だ。そのトップは大臣、府・省の外局である庁のトップは長官と呼ばれる。内閣府以外の大臣がいる省庁を実質的に切り盛りしているのは、**事務次官**という最高位の官僚である。約95万人いるとされる国家公務員の中で各省庁の幹部候補として育成される少数のエリート官僚は、入省３年目で**係長**クラス、40代で**課長**、50代で局長の地位が約束されている。順当な昇進のためには、**省益**になることだけを考えて仕事をすることが**鉄則**である。

政府の編成
Composition of Government

内閣府	The Cabinet Office
外務省	Ministry of Foreign Affairs
法務省	Ministry of Justice
財務省	Ministry of Finance
国土交通省	Ministry of Land, Infrastructure and Transport
経済産業省	Ministry of Economy, Trade and Industry
総務省	Ministry of Internal Affairs and Communications
厚生労働省	Ministry of Health, Labour and Welfare
農林水産省	Ministry of Agriculture, Forestry and Fisheries
文部科学省	Ministry of Education, Culture, Sports, Science and Technology
環境省	Ministry of the Environment
防衛省	Ministry of Defense
国家公安委員会	National Public Safety Commission

Central Administrative Organs

The executive branch governs the country based on the laws and budget passed by the Diet, and responsibility for individual administrative areas is in the hands of the central ministries. At the head of each ministry is a minister, and the head of a special external agency is called a commissioner. Aside from the Cabinet Office, organizations headed by a minister are in reality run by administrative vise ministers, the highest rank in the civil service. Of the 95,000 national civil servants, these vice ministers are among the elite few trained as candidates for upper professional positions. Within three years of entering the ministry, they are virtually guaranteed to rise to a position equivalent to that of a subsection chief, to subsection manager at the age of forty, and to bureau chief at fifty. In order to proceed smoothly up this latter, the ironclad rule is that the good of the ministry must be given priority in all work.

府・省
Cabinet Offices / Ministries

内局
Intra-ministerial Bureau

| 大臣官房 Minister's Secretariat |
| 局 Bureau |
| 部 Department |
| 課 Section |
| 室・係 Office / Subsection |

庁・委員会
Agency / Commission

府・省の下に置かれる庁は外局とされるが、担当大臣がいる金融庁・消費者庁のほか宮内庁、警察庁、検察庁は別格の庁と位置づけられる。なお、2023年創設のこども家庭庁は21番目の庁になる

The bureaus established under the Cabinet Office and the various ministries are called external agencies. In addition to the Financial Services Agency and the Consumer Affairs Agency, which are headed by responsible ministers, special status is held by the Imperial Household Agency, the National Police Agency, and the Public Prosecutor's Office. The Child and Family Agency, to be established in 2023, will be the twenty-first agency.

□政府（行政府） executive branch
□中央官庁 central ministries
□府 Cabinet Office
□省 Ministry
□外局 external agency
□庁 Agency
□切り盛りする run
□事務次官 administrative vise minister
□係長 subsection chief
□課長 subsection manager
□局長 bureau chief
□省益 the good of ministry
□鉄則 ironclad rule

23

官僚制のしくみ

日本の行政官僚は「優秀」である、と言われる。その頂点に立つのが、国家公務員採用総合職試験という最難関をパスして官庁に採用された、ごく一握りの「キャリア」と呼ばれる人たちである。彼らは大多数の「ノン・キャリア」が、30数年かけても到達し得ないポストに数年で楽々と昇り詰めてしまう。例えば、ここで紹介している財務官僚の出世コースに見られるように、キャリアは30歳前後に地方の税務署長になるのである。このような「キャリアの道」は、どの省庁にも存在する。そして、この道を進むには余計なことをしないに限るのである。難問は後続の人に任せ、決められた歩幅で粛々と歩く。その生き方こそが、優秀さの現れなのだ。

□行政官僚 administrative bureaucracy
□頂点 pinnacle
□国家公務員採用総合職試験 National Civil Service Exam for Career-Track Positions
□ごく一握りの a small handful of
□到達し得ない cannot hope to reach

□昇り詰める rise to the top
□出世コース promotion course
□地方の税務署長 head of a Regional Revenue Office
□決められた歩幅 predetermined pace
□粛々と at a steady pace

The administrative bureaucracy of Japan is said to be made up of the "chosen few." At the pinnacle of this class stand the career bureaucrats, a small handful of individuals who are employed by government agencies after passing a rigorous selection process known as the National Civil Service Exam for Career-Track Positions. These career bureaucrats rise with ease to government posts that the much more numerous non-career bureaucrats could not hope to reach even after 30 or more years of service. For example, as can be seen from the promotion course of a Ministry of Finance bureaucrat introduced here, one of career status will become the head of a Regional Revenue Office by the time he or she is around age 30. This kind of career path exists in every ministry of government, and the key to advancing along it is to avoid involvement in troublesome matters. Leave difficult problems to your successors to solve, and plod along the path at a steady, predetermined pace—such is the true measure of bureaucratic excellence.

行政

財務省官僚の出世コース
Career track for Ministry of Finance bureaucrats

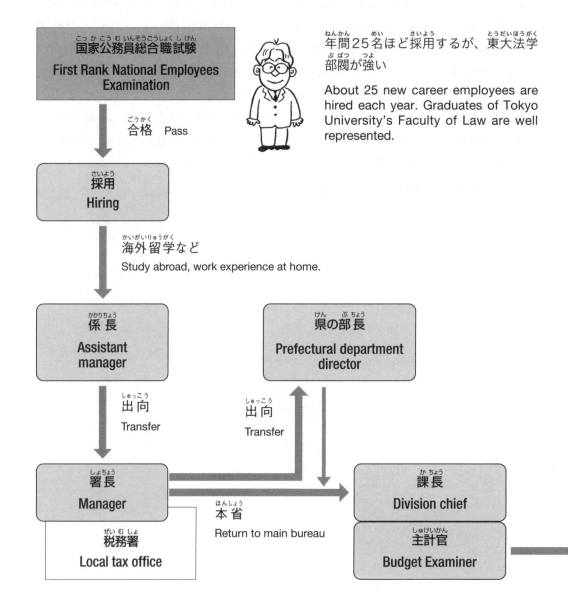

年間25名ほど採用するが、東大法学部閥が強い

About 25 new career employees are hired each year. Graduates of Tokyo University's Faculty of Law are well represented.

国家公務員総合職試験
First Rank National Employees Examination

合格　Pass

採用
Hiring

海外留学など
Study abroad, work experience at home.

係長
Assistant manager

県の部長
Prefectural department director

出向
Transfer

出向
Transfer

署長
Manager

税務署
Local tax office

本省
Return to main bureau

課長
Division chief

主計官
Budget Examiner

事務次官は同期入省者から1名だけ。30年間の次官レースは苛酷である

Only one person out of each incoming class of new career employees can become Administrative Vice-Minister. The thirty-year race to become vice-minister is a tough one.

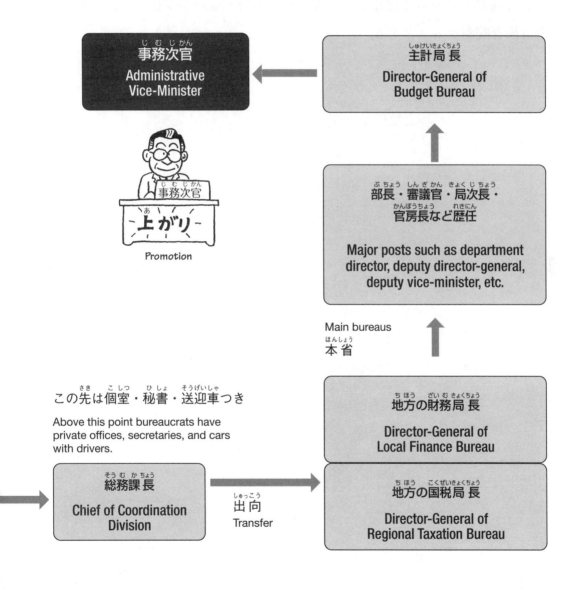

事務次官
Administrative
Vice-Minister

主計局長
Director-General of
Budget Bureau

部長・審議官・局次長・官房長など歴任

Major posts such as department director, deputy director-general, deputy vice-minister, etc.

上がり
Promotion

Main bureaus
本省

この先は個室・秘書・送迎車つき

Above this point bureaucrats have private offices, secretaries, and cars with drivers.

総務課長
Chief of Coordination Division

出向
Transfer

地方の財務局長
Director-General of
Local Finance Bureau

地方の国税局長
Director-General of
Regional Taxation Bureau

□ 事務次官 Administrative Vice-Minister
□ 苛酷 tough

24

行政（ぎょうせい）

予算は、1年間の収入と支出の予定計画であるが、会計年度は4月1日から翌年3月31日までとなっている。ところで予算案は財務省がその実務作業（財務原案）をし、内閣が編成した後に、国会の審議を経て成立。この過程では、各官庁や政治家による虚々実々の予算の分捕り合戦が行われることは、周知のところだ。予算が配分されると各省庁は、3か月ごとに支払い計画書を財務省に提出し、承認されると日本銀行が支払う。決算書は、会計検査院がチェックする。

□収入　income
□支出　expenditure
□会計年度　accounting year
□編成する　compile
□成立する　be enacted

□虚々実々の　diamond cut diamond
□分捕り合戦　tug-of-war
□周知　well-known
□会計検査院　the Board of Audit

Preparing the Budget

The budget is the plan for the government's income and expenditures for the accounting year running from April 1 through the next March 31. The budget proposal is prepared by the Ministry of Finance, compiled by the Cabinet, and discussed and approved by the Diet. While the budget is being prepared, government ministries, agencies, and politicians engage in a fierce tug-of-war over the allocation of funds. After the money been earmarked, each ministry and government agency must submit a spending plan to the Ministry of Finance. After a plan is approved, the Bank of Japan disperses the funds. The records of the expenditures are later checked by the Board of Audit.

Executive Branch

行政（ぎょうせい）

4月（がつ） April
新年度予算見積り（しんねんど よさんみつも）
Budget estimate for new fiscal year
夏（なつ） Summer
予算編成方針発表（よさんへんせいほうしんはっぴょう）
Announcement of policy for compilation of budget

財務省主計局（ざいむしょうしゅけいきょく）

Budget Bureau, Ministry of Finance

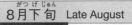

8月下旬（がつげじゅん） Late August

概算要求（がいさんようきゅう）

Requests

Request

各省庁の担当課長が主計局に提出（かくしょうちょう たんとうかちょう しゅけいきょく ていしゅつ）

The division chiefs in government ministries and agencies submit their requests to the Budget Bureau.

Investigator

主査（しゅさ）

Budget Examiner

主計官（しゅけいかん）

査定（さてい） **Assessment**

概算要求（がいさんようきゅう）をもとに**主計官（しゅけいかん）**と**主査（しゅさ）**が中心（ちゅうしん）になって、**予算（よさん）**の**査定（さてい）作業（さぎょう）**をする

The budget examiners and investigators evaluate the budget request.

□主計官 budget examiner   □主査 investigator   □査定をする evaluate

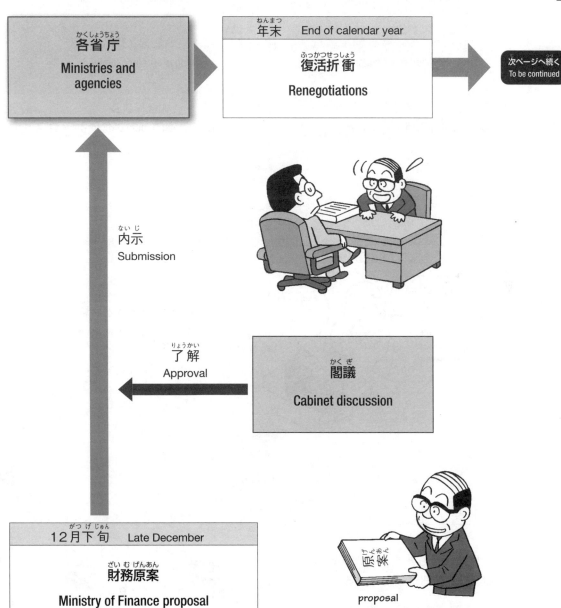

かくしょうちょう
各省庁
Ministries and agencies

ねんまつ
年末 End of calendar year

ふっかつせっしょう
復活折衝

Renegotiations

次ページへ続く
To be continued

ない じ
内示
Submission

りょうかい
了解
Approval

かく ぎ
閣議

Cabinet discussion

がつ げ じゅん
12月下旬 Late December

ざい む げんあん
財務原案

Ministry of Finance proposal

proposal

111

行政

事務折衝
Detailed negotiations

各省課長 Ministerial division chiefs	対 vs.	**主計局主査** Budget Bureau investigators
各省局長 Ministerial bureau chiefs	対 vs.	**主計局主計官** Budget Bureau examiners
各省次官 Administrative vice-ministers	対 vs.	**主計局次長** Budget Bureau Deputy Director-General

大臣折衝
Ministerial negotiations

キミの頼みでもこれだけはダメ！

I just can't agree to this one item.

なんとか頼むよ

Please! I beg of you!

各省庁の大臣と財務大臣
Government ministers and the Minister of Finance

政治折衝
Political bargaining

大臣折衝でも決着がつかない場合は、与党幹部が調整に入る

If the ministers are unable to reach a settlement, three top leaders of the ruling party settle the disputes.

Chief secretary 幹事長

政調会長 Policy chief

General council chairman 総務会長

補正予算
ほ せい よ さん

Additional appropriations

予算成立後に予想しえなかった歳出が
よ さんせいりつ ご   よ そう   さいしゅつ
生じた場合に編成される
しょう ば あい へんせい

Additional appropriations are made
when unexpected expenditures arise
after the budget has been finalized.

本予算の執行は4月1日から
ほん よ さん しっこう   がつ にち
Main budget goes into effect on April 1.

成立
せいりつ

Finalization

暫定予算
ざんてい よ さん

Provisional budget

予算不成立の場合
よ さん ふ せいりつ   ば あい

The provisional budget is used if the
Diet does not approve the budget
proposal.

参議院
さん ぎ いん

House of Councillors

参議院が30日以内に決議しない場合に
さん ぎ いん   にち い ない けつ ぎ   ば あい
は、衆議院の議決が国会の議決となる
しゅう ぎ いん ぎ けつ こっかい ぎ けつ

If the House of Councillors does not reach
a decision within 30 days, the decision of
the lower house becomes final.

決定 Decision
けってい

内閣
ないかく

Cabinet

年末
ねんまつ
End of year

政府案として提出
せい ふ あん   ていしゅつ
Submission of govern-
ment proposal

衆議院
しゅう ぎ いん

House of Representatives

予算案は衆議院が先議する。予算委員会で審議
よ さんあん しゅう ぎ いん せん ぎ   よ さん い いんかい しん ぎ
の後、本会議に上程され、審議・採決される
あと ほんかい ぎ じょうてい   しん ぎ さいけつ

The budget proposal is discussed first by
the House of Representatives. After passing
through the Budget Committee, it goes to the
full Diet, where it is discussed and approved
or rejected.

国債発行のしくみ

◁))） 　国債は政府の借金である。わが国の国家予算は年々増大して年間100兆円規模になっている。にもかかわらず、その財源となる税収は不況のあおりを受けて伸び悩んでいる。本来なら収入（歳入）に応じた支出（歳出）をするのが当然なのだが、その経済原則が通用しないしくみになってしまっているのだ。

　歳出過多をカバーするため、政府は大量の赤字国債（右ページ）を発行し続け、債務（借金）は1255兆円（2022年6月末時点）にのぼる。

We don't have enough money!

お金が足りません！どうしましょう？

国債の目的別分類	Types of Government Bonds
普通国債	Regular bonds
交付国債	Delivery bonds
財投債	Investment-and-loan bonds
借換国債	Refinancing bonds
個人向け国債	Individual bonds

◁))） 外国のグリーン国債と同様の、脱炭素社会に移行させるための資金調達を目的とする「GX経済移行債（仮称）」の発行が検討されている

The issuance of GX Economic Transition Bonds (tentative name), similar to foreign green government bonds, is being considered to finance the transition to a decarbonized society.

☐国債 (government) bonds 　　☐財源 source of funds 　　☐伸び悩む be sluggish

☐国家予算 national budget 　　☐不況 recession 　　☐経済原則 economic principle

Capital Investment- and Deficit-Financing Bonds

Bonds are debts that the government owes. The national budget of Japan now amounts to nearly 100 trillion yen for the fiscal year. In spite of this, tax revenues, which are the government's main source of funds, have suffered due to the recession. One might naturally expect expenditures to stay in line with revenue, but this economic principle no longer applies.

To cover overspending, the government continues to issue a large amount of deficit-covering government bonds (see this page below), and its debt (borrowing) amounts to 1.255 quadrillion yen (as of the end of June 2022).

建設国債
Capital investment financing bonds

国債のうち、住宅や道路などの社会資本をつくる事業資金調達のために発行する国債

These are bonds issued to procure funds for the building of roads, housing, and other kinds of social overhead capital.

赤字国債
Deficit-financing bonds

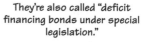
They're also called "deficit financing bonds under special legislation."

建設国債以外の経常的な支出に当てる国債。歳入不足を補填する場合に発行するが、インフレの原因になるため原則的には禁止されている。やむを得ず発行しなければならなくなった場合は、そのつど国会に諮って「特例法」による発行が必要になるため、特例国債とも呼ばれる

Deficit 赤字　特例国債とも呼ばれています　国債

These are bonds issued aside from capital investment financing bonds, to cover ordinary operating expenditures. They are issued in cases where the annual revenue is insufficient, but since they tend to cause inflation, in principle issue of these bonds is prohibited, except in unavoidable situations. Even in such cases, since they can only be issued after deliberation in the Diet and the drafting of a special government order, they are also referred to as "deficit financing bonds under special legislation."

□ 通用しない　no longer applies
□ 歳出過多　overspending
□ 赤字国債　deficit-covering government bond
□ 発行する　issue
□ 社会資本　social overhead capital
□ 調達する　procure

□ 経常的　ordinary
□ 補填する　cover
□ 原則的には　in principle
□ 国会に諮って　after deliberation in the Diet
□ 特例法　special law

26

公共事業のしくみ

行政

国や**地方自治体**が、社会全体の利益のため**公共投資**によって行う事業を公共事業という。大部分は大型建設事業で、予算の省庁別シェアをみると、**国土交通省**はつねに7割近くを占めている。

公共事業は、(1)生活環境整備、(2)**国土保全**、(3)産業基盤整備の3つに大別される。具体的には、道路整備や**港湾**整備、橋や空港などの建設、上下水道や公共施設の建設整備、**治山・治水**、災害復旧などが公共事業に含まれる。そこで動く巨大資金は、直接たずさわる建設業界のみならず、各産業界の活性化にもつながる。不況の際、景気対策の目玉として公共事業の**前倒し**執行によって、景気の**底上げ**を図るのが常だ。

□地方自治体　local government
□公共投資　public investment
□国土交通省　the Ministry of Land, Infrastructure and Transport
□国土保全　preservation of national land
□産業基盤　industrial foundation
□港湾　harbors
□治山・治水　afforestation, flood prevention
□前倒し　front-loading
□底上げ　boost

Public Works

Public works are projects undertaken by national or local governments in the interests of society as a whole, using public investments. The Ministry of Land, Infrastructure and Transport focuses some 70% of the national public works expenditure available to ministries and agencies on large-scale construction works.

Public works are classified broadly into three categories: 1) maintenance of living environments; 2) preservation of national land; and 3) maintenance of industrial foundations. Specifically, public works include the maintenance of roads and harbors, construction of bridges and airports, construction and maintenance of water works and public facilities, afforestation, flood prevention, and post-disaster restoration. The enormous capital that is set in motion leads to the revitalization of not only the construction trade directly involved, but of all areas of industry. During periods of recession, the front-loading of public works generally becomes a focal point in measures to boost the economy.

Executive Branch

公共事業の手順
こうきょうじぎょう てじゅん

Public works procedures

用地確保
ようちかくほ

Procuring of site

設計
せっけい

Drawing up of plan

指名業者選定
しめいぎょうしゃせんてい

Nomination of businesses for contract

入札
にゅうさつ

Tendering

契約
けいやく

Signing of contract

前払い金の支払い
まえばらい きん しはら

Advance payment

施工
せこう

Construction

公共事業の予算執行は、毎年4〜9月と10〜3月の半期ごとに行われる
こうきょうじぎょう よさんしっこう まいとし がつ がつ はんき おこな

Public works budgetary allocations are made semiannually, between April and September, and between October and March.

公共事業の前倒し執行
Front-load implementation of public works

景気を刺激するために、上半期（4～9月）に契約する事業数を増やし、前払い金の支払いを多くする。これによって、民間企業の活性化を図ろうというわけだ

To stimulate the economy, the number of contractors used is increased in the first half of the year (April to September). The consequent boost in advance payments also helps revitalize the private sector.

The cabinet decides the percentage of public works to be carried out.

公共事業の執行率は閣議で決めます

国の公共事業関係費は、国が直接実施する事業のための経費（直轄事業費）と地方自治体が実施する事業を補助する経費（補助事業費）に大別される

Expenditures related to public works can be broadly classified as direct works expenditure (which is the cost of public works under the direct control of the central government) and subsidized project expenditure (which is the cost borne by the central government in projects implemented by local governments).

□ 活性化する revitalize
□ 直轄 direct control
□ 大別される be broadly classified

地方自治のしくみ
ちほうじち

27

◁))) 　いわゆる「平成の大合併」を契機に、日本の基礎自治体数は約3200（1998
年）から1747に激減した（2022年1月時点）。併せて従来、自治体のトップ
「三役」とされていた市町村長、助役、収入役のうち、助役が副市町村
長に呼称変更され、特別職の収入役（都道府県は出納長）が廃止されて一
般職から会計責任者が任命されるようになった。
　これらは国が進めてきた地方分権という権限移譲の一環でもあったが、
それに伴う財源の確保がままならないために苦慮する地方自治体も多い。

区　分
く　ぶん

Administrative Divisions

都	Metropolitan Area	東京	Tokyo
道	Circuit	北海道	Hokkaido
府	Urban Prefectures	京都／大阪	Kyoto/Osaka
県	Prefectures	43県	The 43 Prefectures
市	Cities	一般市・特別区（東京都）の他に、政令指定都市・中核市等を指定 Aside from ordinary cities and those with special status (i.e., Tokyo), there are also ordinance-designated cities and core cities.	
町	Towns	人口5万人未満が原則	
村	Villages	As a rule, having a population of less than 50,000.	

□合併　merger
□市長村長　mayor
□助役　deputy mayor
□副市長村長　assistant mayor
□特別職　specialized government civil servant
□廃止される　be abolished

□一般職　regular (government) service
□地方分権　decentralization
□権限移譲　transfer of authority
□一環　part of
□苦慮する　have trouble
□行財政権　fiscal and administrative power
□交付金　grant-in-aid

Local Self-Government

The so-called Great Merger of the Heisei Era has led to a dramatic decrease in the number of basic local governments in Japan from approximately 3,200 (1998) to 1,747 (as of January 2022). Subsequently, two of the "three top batters" of local government—mayors of cities, towns, and villages; deputy mayors; and treasurers—underwent a change. The deputy mayors were renamed assistant mayors, and treasurers as specialized government civil servants (or bursars in the case of the largest administrative divisions) were abolished and replaced by an accountant appointed from regular government service.

   This was part of a government policy to transfer more administrative power to the local level. Accompanying this is the fact that many local governments are having trouble securing suitable sources of revenue.

Executive Branch

政令指定都市
Ordinance-designated cities

人口50万人以上の都市で、**行財政権**は府県なみ。行政手続き上は、府県を経由しないで**交付金**を受けることができたり、国道を管理できるなど国と直接交渉ができる。20市（2022年）

These are cities with a population of at least 500 thousand, which maintain fiscal and administrative powers equivalent to those held by the prefectures. These cities negotiate directly with the central government in order to receive grants-in-aid, rather than going through the prefectural government. They are also given the power to manage national roadways within their area of jurisdiction. Twenty cities (as of 2022).

The city mayor and prefectural governor are on the same level.

知事と市長は対等

市長 Mayor　知事 Governor

政令都市

中核市
Core Cities

人口20万人以上で、政令指定都市に準じた権限を持つことができる都市。62市（2022年）

These are cities with a population of at least 200 thousand, which maintain autonomous powers similar to those of ordinance-designated cities. Sixty-two cities (as of 2022).

昼間の人口が夜間より多いことも条件！

Another condition is that the daytime population must be larger than the nighttime population.

121

行政

財源
Revenue Sources

地方自治体が、文字通りの**自治体制**を維持するには**財政基盤**の確立が**不可欠**だが、その裏づけとなる自主**財源**の確保は難題である。自治体は住民サービス業であり、サービスの対価はお客である住民から取るしかないが、自ら**徴収**できるのは住民税、事業税、地方消費税などに限られる。

In order for local governments to maintain a true system of self-government, it is essential that they establish a solid financial base. It proves difficult, however, to secure the revenue sources that make this possible. Such local governments must supply necessary services to their citizens and charge them for the cost of such services. But the means of doing this are rather limited—residence taxes, business taxes, consumption taxes, and such.

自主財源 Independent revene sources	住民税 Residence Tax
	事業税 Business Tax
	地方消費税 Local Consumption Tax
	不動産取得税 Real Estate Acquisition Tax
	自動車取得税 Vehicle Acquisition Tax
	使用料・手数料 Usage Fees and Commissions
依存財源 External revenue sources	地方交付税交付金 Local Grants-in-aid and Subsidies
	国庫支出金 Payments from national treasury
	地方譲与税 Local transfer taxes
	地方債 Local bonds

財政健全化指標
Index of Financial Health

俗に“3割自治”といわれるように、財源の大半を地方交付税交付金や国庫支出金などに依存してきた体質を、急に変えろといわれても困ってしまうだけである。政府は毎年、地方自治体の財政破綻の予防措置として「財政健全化指標」の公表を義務づけているが、財政再建団体に指定されると住民サービスの劣化をよぎなくされる。

As indicated by the saying, "30% local," which means that only 30% of local revenue comes from local sources, the majority of revenue is provided by grants-in-aid, subsidies, and treasury disbursements from the central government. Having long relied on this system, local governments find it difficult to suddenly change. For its part, as a means of preventing local fiscal bankruptcy, the central government has established an index of financial health that must be made public every year. But once a locality has been designated "an organization for fiscal reconstruction," public services inevitably deteriorate.

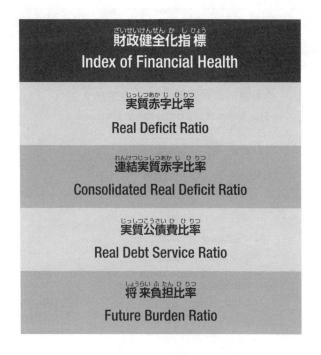

財政健全化指標
Index of Financial Health

実質赤字比率
Real Deficit Ratio

連結実質赤字比率
Consolidated Real Deficit Ratio

実質公債費比率
Real Debt Service Ratio

将来負担比率
Future Burden Ratio

実質公債費（借金）比率が35％超は、財政再建団体として認定され、政府の管理下に置かれる

If the real debt service ratio exceeds 35%, the local government in question is designated an Organization for Fiscal Reconstruction and placed under the supervision of the central government.

□ 自治 self-government

□ 財政基盤 solid financial basis

□ 確立する establish

□ 不可欠 essential

□ 財源 revenue source

□ 徴収する collect

□ 俗に commonly

□ 地方交付税交付金 local allocation tax grants

□ 国庫支出金 national treasury disbursements

□ 財政破綻 fiscal bankruptcy

□ 公表する make public

□ 財政再建団体 organization for fiscal reconstruction

□ 劣化をよぎなくされる inevitably deteriorate

公務員処分のしくみ

28

国家公務員は「国民全体の**奉仕者**として、公共の利益のために勤務し、**且つ**、職務の遂行に当たっては、全力を挙げてこれに専念しなければならない」と法律に定められている。そして、その義務として職務専門義務、守秘義務、政治活動の禁止がうたわれている。この規定に違反した場合、制裁として以下のような処分が課されるのである。

しかし、処分決定の権限は各機関の長にあるので、とかく**身内**に**甘く**なってしまう傾向が強い。口頭注意、厳重注意、訓告でお茶を濁してしまうケースが多いのもそのためだ。

国家公務員のケース

National government employees

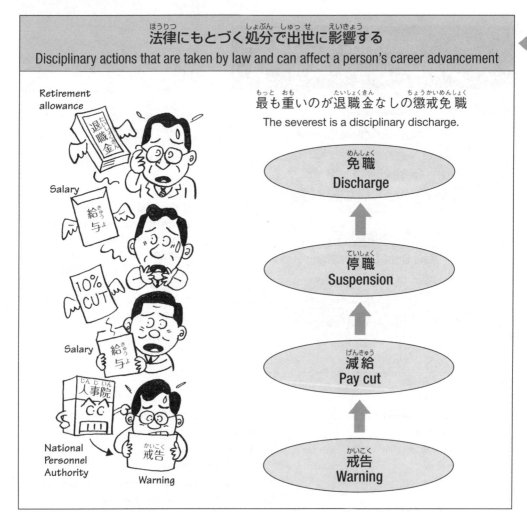

法律にもとづく処分で出世に影響する

Disciplinary actions that are taken by law and can affect a person's career advancement

Retirement allowance
退職金
Salary
給与
10% CUT
Salary
給与
人事院
National Personnel Authority
戒告
Warning

最も重いのが退職金なしの懲戒免職

The severest is a disciplinary discharge.

免職
Discharge

↑

停職
Suspension

↑

減給
Pay cut

↑

戒告
Warning

Disciplining Public Servants

Employees of the national government are, by law, servants of the people who work for the public benefit and make every effort to carry out their assigned tasks. Their obligations include giving doing their best at work, maintaining confidentiality, and not participating in political activities. If they violate any of these rules, they can be disciplined as shown below.

The power to take disciplinary action is held by the heads of government organizations who tend to be lenient on their colleagues. That's why so many cases are settled with merely a verbal warning, admonition or reprimand.

人事院
National Personnel Authority

内閣の統括のもとに置かれ、公務員の人事行政全般にわたり独立した準立法および準司法機能をもつ機関。処分に不服の場合は、「救済の審判」を申し立てることができる

The National Personnel Authority is controlled by the Cabinet. It has quasi legislative and judicial powers over all personnel matters concerning public servants. Employees who are unhappy with the decision can appeal for a hearing.

処分
Disciplinary action

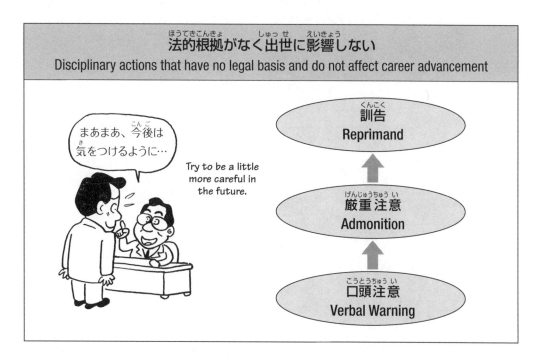

法的根拠がなく出世に影響しない
Disciplinary actions that have no legal basis and do not affect career advancement

まあまあ、今後は気をつけるように…

Try to be a little more careful in the future.

訓告
Reprimand

厳重注意
Admonition

口頭注意
Verbal Warning

□奉仕者 servant
□且つ and
□身内 colleague

□甘い lenient
□準立法および準司法機能 quasi legislative and judicial powers

第3章 暮らし

ざっくり読んでも役に立つ
This is well-worth a look

29

日本銀行のしくみ

暮らし

　日本の**中央銀行**としての日本銀行は、国内外に対する**金融政策**のコントロール・タワーである。その柱の一つが**公開市場操作**で、民間の**金融機関**が持っている国債などを売買することで市場に流れるお金を調整している。経済不況は**お金が回らなくなる**ことを意味するが、そんな時、日銀は市場に大量にお金を供給する必要がある。しかし、供給し過ぎると、お金の価値が下がるインフレを招くため、調整は困難を極める。

　日本銀行は、銀行のための銀行である。金融機関にお金が不足すると、貸し出しをする。その場合、国債が**担保**とされることが多い。そして日銀から安い金利で借りたお金を、企業や市民に**また貸し**して、**利ざや**を稼ぐのが市中銀行である。その市中銀行が経営破綻になったら、預金者保護の**名目**で日銀は「**特融**」という、事実上は無担保の貸し出しができる。

□中央銀行　central bank
□金融政策　monetary policy
□公開市場操作　open market operation
□金融機関　financial institution
□お金が回らなくなる　money is stagnating

□担保　security
□また貸しする　subletting
□利ざや　interest
□〜の名目で　in the name of
□特融　special loan

The Bank of Japan

As the central bank of Japan, the Bank of Japan is the control tower for monetary policy both in Japan and abroad. One of its chief means of doing this is open market operations: the Bank buys and sells government bonds etc. held by private financial institutions and in that way adjusts the market money flow. A recession means that the movement of money is stagnating, and this calls for the Bank to inject large amounts of money into the market. However, if this is done to excess, the value of money drops and invites inflation, demonstrating the difficulty of such operations.

The Bank of Japan is a bank for banks. When money becomes scarce the Bank of Japan lends money to financial institutions. Security usualy consists of government bonds. Money borrowed at low interest from the Bank of Japan is then lent out to private corporations and citizens, and the interest on these loans is pocketed by commercial banks. If a commercial bank goes bankrupt, the Bank of Japan provides loans (*tokuyū*) without security in the interests of protecting depositors.

日銀本店
The Head Office of the Bank of Japan

政策委員会（定員9名）
The Policy Committee (nine members)

日銀の最高議決機関である。総裁、副総裁、都銀・地銀代表、財務省・経済企画庁の政府代表で構成。政府代表には議決権がない

This is the highest authority within the Bank of Japan, and comprises the Governor and Deputy-Governor of the bank, city and country bank representatives, as well as government representatives from the Ministry of Finance and the Economic Planning Agency. The government representatives, however, have no resolution-making power.

役員会
The Executive Assembly

他に審議委員・理事等15名以内と参与（若干名）

In addition, there are up to 15 members of the policy board and executive directors. There can also be a few additional consultants.

総裁
Governor

副総裁（2名）
Deputy-Governor
(two members)

総裁・副総裁・審議委員（6名）は、内閣が任命。総裁は大蔵省（現・財務省）と日銀出身者が占めてきたが、2023年4月に就任した植田和男総裁（第32代）は学者出身

The Governor and Deputy-Governor are appointed by the Cabinet. The governor has come from the ministry of Finance or from within the Bank of Japan. But Ueda Kazuo, whose term as 32nd governor of the Bank of Japan began in April 2023, has an academic background.

本店は２室・12局と金融研究所がある

The head office comprises two offices, 12 departments, and the Institute for Monetary and Economic Studies.

支店（全国32か所）

Branch offices (32 nationwide)

国内事務所（14か所）＊電算センター含む

14 local offices in Japan
(Including a central data processing center in Fuchu)

海外駐在員事務所（7か所）

Overseas representative office

ニューヨーク・ワシントン・ロンドン・北京・香港・パリ・フランクフルトに駐在員を派遣している

The Bank of Japan has overseas representative offices in New York, Washington, London, Beijing, Hong Kong, Paris, and Frankfurt.

日銀はその中立性を守るため、政府から独立した特殊法人である

In order to protect its neutrality, the Bank of Japan has the status of a special corporate body independent of the government.

- □ 総裁 Governor
- □ 副総裁 Deputy-Governor
- □ 都銀・地銀代表 city and country bank representative
- □ 経済企画庁 Economic Planning Agency
- □ 議決権 resolution-making power
- □ 理事 director
- □ 参与 consultant
- □ 特殊法人 special corporate body

暮らし

日本銀行
The Bank of Japan

市中銀行は日銀への当座預金を義務づけられていて、その残高が多いほど資金に余裕があることを示す

Commercial banks are required to maintain a current account at the Bank of Japan, and the greater the deposit balance, the greater the funds available to the Bank of Japan.

貸し出し
Loan

預金
Deposit
返済
Repayment

市中銀行
Commercial Banks

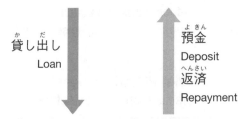

bank book
通帳

○○銀行

八百屋

vegetable shop

貸し出し
Loan

払い戻し
Reimbursement

預金
Deposit
返済
Repayment

Daily Life

特融
BOJ Loan

法律上、特融という言葉はないが、旧日銀法25条の条文にもとづくため、内部では「25条貸し出し」と呼ばれている。これが**発動される**見返りに、破綻金融機関には「業務停止命令」が出される

A Bank of Japan loan (tokuyū) is officially referred to as Article 25 of The Lending Policy, based on the original Bank of Japan Law. When this is invoked, bankrupt financial institutions file for a Suspension of Operations Order.

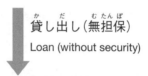

貸し出し（無担保）
Loan (without security)

経営危機の金融機関
Endangered Financial Institution

2011年3月の東日本大震災の直後、日銀が供給した資金は約100兆円にのぼる。さらに日銀は、被災地の金融機関を対象に総額1兆円を低利で貸し出すこととした

Immediately after the Eastern Japan Earthquake Disaster of March 2011, the Bank of Japan injected as much as 100 trillion yen into the money market. Going a step further, the Bank decided to make soft loans of 1 trillion yen available to local financial institutions.

□ 当座預金 current account
□ 残高 deposit balance
□ 発動される be invoked
□ 業務停止命令 Suspention of Operations Order

暮らし

🔊 株式の売買は**証券会社**を通じて、**証券取引所**などの**証券市場**で行うのが一般的である。かつては東京・大阪・名古屋が三大証券取引所とされていたが、2013年に東京・大阪が経営統合されて**持株会社**の日本取引所グループが発足した。

そして2022年4月、東京証券取引所において新たな市場区分での取引がスタートした。**プライム市場**、**スタンダード市場**、**グロース市場**である。ちなみに最上位のプライム市場では、**流通株式**比率35％以上で**時価総額**100億円以上が求められる。

株式は**有価証券**なので、現金と同様の扱いを受ける。通常、証券会社を通じて株式を売買する場合は「**保護預かり条約**」を結んで口座を開く。株式を売却するとキャピタルゲイン税、消費税などがかかる。

しかし、金融ビッグバンの本格化で、**有価証券取引税**が**撤廃され**、99年10月からは**委託手数料**が完全自由化された。そこで、従来の手数料をゼロにする会社やインターネット取引で新規参入を図る会社も現れ、株式売買の世界は競争が激化している。

□証券会社 securities company
□証券取引所 stock exchange
□証券市場 securities market
□持株会社 holding company
□プライム市場 Prime Market
□スタンダード市場 Standard Market
□グロース市場 Growth Market

□流通株式 tradable share
□時価総額 market capitalization
□有価証券 securities
□保護預かり条約 protection safekeeping contract
□有価証券取引税 tax on securities
□撤廃される be abolished
□委託手数料 consignment fee

Buying and Selling Stocks

Stocks are generally traded through a securities company on a securities market, such as a stock exchange. Tokyo, Osaka, and Nagoya used to be the three major stock exchanges, but in 2013, Tokyo and Osaka merged to form a holding company called the Japan Exchange Group.

In April 2022, the Tokyo Stock Exchange started using new market trading segments. These are the Prime Market, the Standard Market, and the Growth Market. Incidentally, the Prime Market, the highest level, requires a minimum of 35% of tradable shares and a market capitalization of at least 10 billion yen.

Stocks are securities, and can thus be treated in the same way as money. Normally, when stocks are bought and sold through securities companies, an account is opened with what is called a "protection safekeeping contract," and when stocks are sold, capital gains and consumption taxes are levied.

However, in the wake of Japan's Big Bang, taxes on securities were abolished, as were fixed consignment fees. Thus, there are companies that have reduced consignment fees in October 1999 to zero, or that use Internet services to attract new buyers, ushering in phase of intense competition in the area of buying and selling stocks.

Daily Life

上場株
Listed stocks

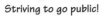

Striving to go public!

上場を目指すぞ！

成長企業

Growing companies

証券取引所で売買されている株で、一定の基準（上場基準）をクリアすることが条件。上場することで企業の社会的信用が増す、資金調達や増資・起債に有利などのメリットがあるため、成長企業は上場を目標とする

Companies must comply with a set of conditions to be listed on the exchange market. Being listed improves the social status of the company, raises capital, and makes it easier to get financing, and so many growing companies strive to go public.

上場・売買
Listing and transactions

証券取引所
Securities exchange

圧倒的な取引額を誇る東京証券取引所以外の国内取引所は、名古屋・札幌・福岡の3か所である。名古屋でも2022年4月から新たな市場区分（プレミア市場、メイン市場、ネクスト市場）に移行した

Other than the Tokyo Stock Exchange, which boasts an overwhelming volume of transactions, there are three other domestic exchanges in Japan: Nagoya, Sapporo, and Fukuoka. Nagoya also shifted to new market classifications (Premier, Main, and Next) in April 2022.

売買
Transactions

証券会社
Securities companies

□ 上場基準 listing criteria
□ 上場する be listed
□ 社会的信用 social credibility
□ 資金調達する get financing
□ 増資・起債する raising capital

□ 非上場 unlisted
□ 日本証券業協会 Japan Securities Dealers Association
□ あえてしない dare not
□ 上場廃止した銘柄 delisted stock

□ 私設取引システム proprietary trading system (PTS)
□ 規制緩和 deregulation
□ 撤退 withdrawal

暮らし

Daily Life

店頭株
Over-the-counter stocks

Listed stocks
上場株

Over-the-counter stocks

店頭株

ちょっと
ハードルが
高いからなあ

"What a high hurdle!"

非上場で、日本証券業協会に登録してい
る株。取引は証券会社の店頭で行われること
からこう呼ばれる。登録基準は上場基準より
はるかに緩いが、あえて上場しない企業もあ
る。上場廃止した銘柄は管理銘柄としてここ
に登録される

Over-the-counter stocks are unlisted, but recorded with the Japan Securities Dealers Association. They get their name because the shares are bought and sold over-the-counter at securities companies. Getting shares on the over-the-counter market is much easier than getting them listed, but some companies prefer over-the-counter shares. Shares taken off the exchange markets are also recorded on the over-the-counter market as controlled shares.

登録
Registration

日本証券業協会
Japan Securities Dealers Association

証券取引所を通さずに株式を売買する「私設取引システム（PTS）」の規制緩和
がされたのは2012年だが、取引量の低迷で撤退が相次ぎ残ったのは2社のみ。
2022年6月、デジタル証券売買の普及をめざして大阪デジタルエクスチェン
ジが開業し、PTS分野へ名乗りを上げた

In 2012, restrictions on proprietary trading systems (PTS), which allow stocks to be bought and sold without going through a stock exchange, were removed, but only two securities companies remained after a string of withdrawals due to sluggish trading volume. In June 2022, Osaka Digital Exchange opened with the aim of popularizing digital securities trading, and entered the PTS field.

暮らし

注文 Order
成行注文 **No limit order**
そのときの相場での売買を依頼 Entrusting the stockbroker to buy or sell stock at his or her discretion.
指値注文 **Limit order**
値段を指定して売買を依頼 Entrusting the broker to buy or sell stock at a set price.
計らい注文 **Discretionary order**
指定した値幅内での売買を依頼 Entrusting the broker to buy or sell stock within a given range of price fluctuations.

◁))

株式を売買するときは、証券会社の窓口で注文する。売買単位は例外もあるが、100株単位である。買いの場合は、「買付概算代金」を預け入れる。注文するときは売買の期限を指定しておくべきだ

Requests for the exchange of stocks are done at the securities company teller's window. While there are exceptions, the standard unit is 100 shares. When shares are purchased, an estimate of purchase form (*kaitsuke gaisan daikin*) is filled out, a deposit is made, and the period of trade is designated.

□ 値幅 range of price fluctuations   □ 正味金額 actual cost
□ 単位 unit   □ 売却代金 sales proceeds
□ 買付概算 estimate of purchase

売買成立確認
Confirmation of transaction

売買が成立した日を「約定日」という

The transaction day is referred to as the pay date.

売買が成立すると「売買報告書」が送られてくるので、内容を確認する

Once a transaction has been concluded, a transaction report is submitted for confirmation.

約定日から4日目に精算する

Accounts must be settled within four days of the transaction day.

精算
Settling of accounts

買い Buying	売り Selling
「買付概算代金」と正味金額の差額を精算し、株券を受け取る Once the difference between the rough estimate and the actual cost is calculated, the stock is received.	「売却代金」を受け取る。これは自宅や、どこでもできる A sales proceeds (*baikyaku daikin*) are received. This can be done from home or anywhere else.

売買委託手数料を支払う
Transaction fees are paid

暮らし

証券会社
Securities company

証券セールスマンは「証券外務員資格試験」の合格者で、この資格がないと売買業務はできない

A certified securities company salesman must have passed the *Shōken Gaimuin Shikaku* examination before conducting any stockrelated business.

Now is the time to buy.

今が買いどきです

I would like to buy 20 shares of Company A

A社の株20株買いたいんですが

ホームトレード
Home trade

自宅から電話を使って株価照会をしたり、売買ができる

Inquiries concerning stocks, as well as their purchase and sale, can be conducted privately by individuals over the telephone.

オンライントレード
Online trading

インターネットを利用して売買を行うシステムで、ネット株取引とも呼ばれる。これが通常の売買と違う点は、取引ごとに必要な手数料が大幅に安くなることで、無料の証券会社もある。利用するには証券会社のホームページで口座を開設することが必要

The system for trading securities via the Internet is also known as Internet trading. The difference between it and ordinary trading is that the fee for individual transactions is much lower, with some exchanges even charging nothing at all. To make use of this system, all you need to do is visit the site of the exchange and open an account.

個人間の売買も可
Individual buying and selling are also permitted

証券会社への手数料が
節約できる

This eliminates the need to
pay securities company fees.

I'll buy that. 買います

I'll sell this.

売ります

個人間の売買での留意事項
Points to be noted by individuals buying and selling stocks

◁))

譲渡 Transfers	個人間で株式を譲渡する場合は「譲渡証書」を作成する必要がある。この証書作成の際は大蔵省令で記載すべき事項が定められているので、それに基づいて行わなければならない When stocks are transferred between individuals, a Ministry of Finance transfer deed is required to which adherence is mandatory.
贈与 Donations and gifts	売買した価格が時価よりもかなり安い場合は、贈与とみなされ贈与税の対象となる When the buying/selling price of the stock is lower than the current going rate, the stock is treated as a donation so gift tax is levied.

- □ 株価照会　inquiries concerning stocks
- □ 譲渡証書　transfer deed
- □ 時価　current going rate
- □ 贈与　donation
- □ 贈与税　gift tax

31

雇用調整のしくみ

暮らし

🔊 日本の伝統的な雇用形態である"終身雇用"が、崩壊しつつある。それどころか、企業では厳しい経済情勢を背景に、人員整理や労働条件の改変すら常態化している風潮さえ見受けられる。

企業にとっては、"会社の存続"という大義のほうが"人"より優先する、つまり会社あってこそ働けるのではないかとの論法である。一方、社員の側は、働く人間がいなければ会社は成り立たないと主張する。

この論議は、常に堂々巡りなのだ。会社員なら、いつ何どき、わが身にふりかかってくるかもしれないのが雇用調整だ。

給与条件変更
Changing Salary Conditions

時短・一時休業 Shortened hours and temporary shutdowns	残業・休日出勤の廃止。休業の場合は平均賃金の6割以上を支払い自宅待機をさせる Abolishment of overtime and work on vacation days. In the case of a temporary shutdown, 60% of a normal salary is paid.
賃金カット Cut in wages	ボーナスや諸手当のみ。給与は本人の同意なしにカットできない Only bonuses and various allowances. Salaries cannot be cut without employee approval.

就労形態変更
Changes in form of employment

配置転換 Employee Reshuffling	雇用契約の範囲内なら本人の同意は不要 If it is within the terms of the employment contract, the employee's agreement is not needed.
出向 Transfer to a subsidiary company	身分・待遇の保証があれば本人の同意は不要 If rank and working conditions are guaranteed, the employee's agreement is not needed.
転籍 Transfer of family register	本人の同意が必要 The employee's approval is needed.

Employment Adjustment

The traditional pattern of employment in Japan, "lifetime employment," is slowly collapsing. In fact, against the backdrop of severe economic times, companies are routinely making personnel cuts and even altering working conditions.

For these companies, their continued corporate existence assumes priority over "people." Their argument is that it is only because of the company's existence that people are able to work. On the other hand, employees stress the point that it is only because of the presence of workers that the company is able to exist.

These two arguments go around and around in a continuous circle. If you are an employee, the possibility of being fired is continually hanging over your head.

整理解雇
Termination due to Restructuring

経営上、客観的な必要があり、社員または労働組合への事前説明・協議がある場合に認められる

This type of dismissal is permitted if an objective reason exists from a business point of view and if the employee or labor union as been consulted and informed of the situation beforehand.

退職勧奨
Suggested early retirement

社内公募 Soliciting within the company	希望退職者には、退職金に**割増賃金**をつけて提示 Aside from severance pay, augmented wages are proposed to those interested in early retirement.
肩たたき Suggesting someone retire early	上司が部下に対して、個別に早期退職を奨める A boss suggests to a subordinate that he personally go into early retirement.

- □ 終身雇用 lifetime employment
- □ 崩壊する collapse
- □ 背景 backdrop
- □ 人員整理 personnel cut
- □ 労働条件 working condition
- □ 常態化している routinely
- □ 存続する continue
- □ 大義 justice
- □ 論法 argument
- □ 堂々巡り go around and around in a continuous circle
- □ 雇用調整 employment adjustment
- □ 諸手当 various allowances
- □ 割増賃金 augmented wage

143

企業倒産

企業の**倒産**には、**再建型**と**清算型**がある。2000年4月施行の「**民事再生法**」は、企業の再建を図る新しい法手続きとして制定された。株式会社・有限会社・医療法人・学校法人などの法人のみならず**個人事業主**にも適用される。法人の場合、再生計画の認可には、出席**債権者**の過半数（届出債権額の2分の1）の同意が必要になる。

近年、**顕著**になっているのが"**後継者難倒産**"である。高齢の経営者に代わる人材がいないため、**放置**しておくと倒産に至るというわけだ。少子高齢化時代ならではの新たな倒産の形といえるだろう。

再建型
Readjustment variants

民事再生 Civil Rehabilitation	裁判所の関与のもとで債権者の協力を得て、事業または経済生活の再生を図る
企業が資金繰りなど**経済的窮地**に陥った場合 When a company encounters economic difficulties due to bad money flow or other reasons.	It tries to restructure its business or economic activity through the intervention of a court of law and the cooperation of its creditors.
会社更生 Corporate Rehabilitation	債権者や株主の利害を調整しながら、管財人が立てた更正計画によって再建を図る
株式会社を対象とし、役員の**総退陣**が前提 Targeting the joint-stock company, it is assumed that corporate executives will be dismissed.	While controlling the concerns of the creditors and stockholders, official receivers consider readjustment possibilities according to rehabilitation plans.

□ 倒産 bankruptcy
□ 再建 restructuring
□ 清算 liquidation
□ 民事再生法 the Civil Rehabilitation Act
□ 個人事業主 self-employed individual

□ 債権者 creditor
□ 顕著 conspicuous
□ 後継者難 lack of successors
□ 放置する be left unchecked
□ 経済的窮地 economic difficulties

□ 裁判所 a court of law
□ 債権者 creditor
□ 総退陣 general resignation
□ 管財人 official receiver
□ 財産配分 to distribute corporate assets

暮らし

Corporate Bankruptcy

There are two types of corporate bankruptcy: debt restructuring and liquidation. The Civil Rehabilitation Act of April 2000 established a new means for corporate restructuring. It applies not only to joint stock corporations, limited liability companies, medical corporations, and educational foundations, but to self-employed individuals as well. For a restructuring plan to be approved, the approval of a majority of creditors (one-half of the registered debt) is needed.

In recent years, "bankruptcy due to lack of successors" has become increasingly conspicuous. There is no one to replace the elderly managers, and if the problem is left unchecked, the company will go bankrupt. This is a new form of bankruptcy that can only occur in an age of declining birthrates and aging population.

清算型
Liquidation variants

管財人が見つからなかったり、更正計画が裁判所に認可されない場合、破産手続きに移行する

In cases in which an official receiver cannot be found, or in which plans for rehabilitation are not recognized by the court, the process of filing for bankruptcy is initiated.

破産
Insolvency

裁判所の宣告により財産を配分し、企業を清算

In accordance with the court's sentence, corporate assets are distributed and the corporation is liquidated.

特別清算
Special Liquidation

裁判所の監督下で財産を配分し、企業を清算

Under the supervision of the court, corporate assets are distributed and the corporation is liquidated.

自主的に企業の解散を裁判所に申し出るもので、債権者との間に財産配分の合意がある場合

Proposals to dissolve a corporation are brought to court independently, and an understanding is made between creditors to distribute corporate assets.

145

宝くじのしくみ

32

暮らし

◁ゆ）　宝くじは、全国都道府県および政令指定都市によって発売され、金融機関によって販売代行される。まず、発行元の自治体が年間の発売計画を議会にかけ、了承を得る。次に**総務省**に発売計画を申請し許可を得た時点で、**受託金融機関を公募する**。受託銀行は、地方自治体の販売計画にそって**公告**し、売りさばき人に販売を**委託する**。売りさばき人は街頭などの宝くじ販売所で、券を販売するというプロセスを経る。

　　購入した**宝くじの当選発表**は新聞などで行われ、当選券は受託銀行で当選金と交換される。「**宝くじ世論調査**」によると、年間100億円もの賞金が、引取人もなく1年の**時効**期間を過ぎて発売元の地方自治体に納付され、公共事業に役立てられているそうだ。

□総務省　Ministry of Internal Affairs and Communications
□受託金融機関　trustee financial institution
□公募する　recruit
□公告する　give public notice

□委託する　entrust
□宝くじの当選発表　lottery winner announcement
□宝くじ世論調査　white paper on lotteries
□時効　statute of limitations

Lotteries

Lottery tickets are sold in all prefectures and in specified cities through financial institutions. Each individual local government submits a sales plan to its council for approval. Upon receiving approval, it recruits financial institutions that then give public notice, select and entrust the lottery sellers in accordance with the sales plan. Those who wish to buy lottery tickets can find stands on the street and elsewhere.

Winning numbers are made public in the newspaper, and the winning lottery tickets are cashed in at specified banks. According to a white paper on lotteries, local governments annually profit some 10 billion yen from lottery tickets that are not cashed in.

暮
ら
し

Lottery stand

宝くじ売場

ジャンボ宝くじ発売中

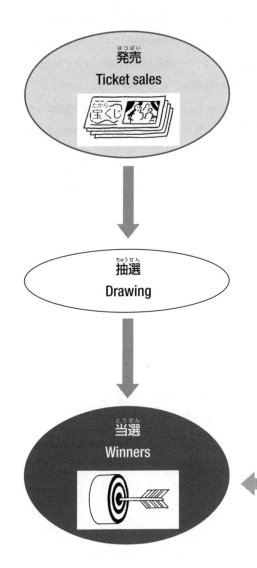

発売
Ticket sales

抽選
Drawing

当選
Winners

数字選択式の宝くじとして、ナンバーズ（2種類）、ミニロト、ロト（2種類）、スクラッチ、ビンゴ5も発売されている

As forms of lottery involving the selection of numbers, NUMBERS (2 types), Mini Loto, Loto (2 types), Scratch and Bingo 5 are available.

当選金の時効は1年間
Winning tickets are valid for one year.

売場で受け取れる当選金は1万円以下（一部の指定売場で5万円以下）である

Tickets that qualify for winnings of 10,000 yen or less (50,000 yen or less at some stands) can be cashed in at the lottery stands.

宝くじ 1 枚当たりのお金の配分比率
Distribution ratio of ticket sales

くじ売場には、売りさばき手数料と当選金支払い手数料が入る

Lottery stands receive sales fees and payout fees.

ジャンボ宝くじ 1 等当選の確率 1/2000万

Probability of winning first prize of a jumbo lottery drawing: 1 in 20 million.

"I just know I'm going to win."

ワクワクドキドキ

宝くじ

最高額
Winning tickets

1等7億円＋前後賞（各1.5億円）

Grand prize worth 700,000,000 yen + one number off, 150,000,000 yen each

10億円
1,000,000,000 yen

その他　約7.5%
Other: 7.5%

自治体の収益金
約39.6%

Profit to the local government: about 39.6%

くじ売場　約9.1%
Lottery stands: About 9.1%

当選金　約43.8%

Winnings: about 43.8%

宝くじの番号は100000番から199999番を1組としている。

そして、01組100000番の**前後賞**は100001番と199999番というように、組の中から出ることになっている

The lottery numbers for each group range from 100000 to 199999.
Some of the winning numbers have runner-up prizes. So if in group 1 the winning number is 100000, the runner-up prizes will go to the holders of the tickets numbered 100001 and 199999.

□前後賞　prize for adjacent numbers

医療費のしくみ

33

暮らし

◁))) 　国民皆保険制度を原則とする日本では、受診するときに保険証を提出すれば保険診療を受けることができる。この場合の医療費を診療報酬といい、医療行為を点数で計算する方法がとられている。診療報酬は、厚生労働大臣が中央社会保険医療協議会（中医協）に諮問したうえで決定される。

　これは出来高によって支払われるため、ともすると医療機関側が請求額を増やそうとして過剰医療を行いがちな点が指摘されてきた。患者側も自己負担分以外の医療費については無関心であるところから、濫診乱療の温床となっていることも見逃せない。また、歯科材料代・差額ベッド代という名目による医療費の差額徴収は、法律上は問題視される。

□国民皆保険制度 a policy of universal health care
□保険診療 health care services provided by health insurance
□診療報酬 medical compensation
□諮問 consult
□出来高 piece-rate

□過剰 excessive
□濫診乱療 over treatment
□温床 hotbed
□差額ベッド代 amenity bed charge
□名目 nominal

Medical Expenses

Japan has a policy of universal health care. Health care services are provided through health insurance. In this system, medical expenses are referred to as medical compensation, and a points system is used for calculating the medical treatment. Proof of insurance is submitted when receiving medical care, and the medical compensation is decided after the Minister of Health, Labour and Welfare consults the Central Social Insurance Medical Council (CSIMC).

It has been pointed out that medical institutions tend to provide excessive medical treatment in order to make the amount of medical compensation as high as possible. This is aggravated by the fact that patients only care about individually paid medical expenses, making medical institutions notable hotbeds of over treatment. Also legally problematic is the fact that patients pay the difference on nominal medical expenses such as dental material charges and the amenity bed charge.

暮らし

医療費支払いのプロセス
Paying medical expenses

病院と開業医では料金体系が異なる

The fee structure at hospitals and private practices.

自己負担分支払い

Portion of medical expense to be paid individually

被保険者
Insured individual

保険料支払い

Payment of insurance expense

保険者 **Insurer**	国や健保組合など National or Health Insurance Union, etc.

請求
Claim

支払い
Payment

支払基金・国保連
Payment Fund/National Insurance Alliance

保険者から審査・支払い業務を委託された機関

Institution entrusted with the investigation and payment from the insurer.

◁))

医療費のうち薬剤費の割合は3割強で、70歳以上の外来患者は5割以上を占める

Drug costs are more than 30 percent of medical expenses, and over 50 percent for outpatients over 70 years old.

病院などの保険診療医療機関
Hospitals and other medical service providers

診療報酬請求

Claim for medical compensation

◁))

レセプト
Rezept

医療機関の請求明細書。1か月単位で提出される。97年に厚生労働省は保険者が被保険者にレセプトを開示する方針を打ち出したが、対応はまちまちだ

A medical institution's bill of particulars that is submitted on a monthly basis. In 1997, the Ministry of Health, Labour and Welfare effected a policy whereby insurers disclose the Rezept to the insured, but compliance has been mixed.

診療報酬支払い

Payment of medical compensation

34

介護保険のしくみ

◁))) **寝たきり**や**認知症**で介護が必要になった場合に備えた**公的**介護保険制度。介護が必要な高齢者にどの程度のサービスを提供するかを決める「**要介護認定**」を経て、「介護サービス計画(ケアプラン)」にもとづく制度である。

サービスは、自立・**要支援**1、2・**要介護**1〜5までの8ランクに分けて判定されるが、自立と判断された場合は給付を受けられない。65歳未満40歳以上の人でも、**パーキンソン病**や**慢性関節リウマチ**などの**特定疾病**は受給 対象となる。公的介護保険の保険料は、市区町村によって若干異なる。

暮らし

□寝たきり bedridden
□認知症 senile dementia
□公的 public
□要介護認定 certification of long-term care need
□要支援 needy of support

□要介護 needy of care
□パーキンソン病 Parkinson's disease
□慢性関節リウマチ rheumatoid arthritis
□特定疾病 special illnesses

Long-term Care Insurance

The Long-term Care Insurance System was initiated for the care of the bedridden and those with senile dementia. It is based on the Care Plan, which consists of a care certification system under which a doctor decides how much medical care each elderly person needs.

The elderly are classified into eight categories: independent, needy of support (levels 1 to 2), and needy of care (levels 1 to 5), with no allowance for those classified as independent. Those between 40 and 65 years of age with Parkinson's disease, rheumatoid arthritis, and other special illnesses also qualify to receive payment. The premium for this new health insurance varies slightly by city, ward, town, and village.

暮らし

公的介護保険制度
Long-term Care Insurance

40歳以上の人に加入を義務付ける公的介護保険制度
は、2000年4月から施行

Everyone over 40 must make payments into the Long-term
Care Insurance System, implemented in April 2000.

財源 Revenue
市町村が制度運営者となり、 介護特別会計を設定する Cities, towns and villages operate the system and have special medical care accounting departments.

▶

指定機関へ介護保険報酬の支払い Payment to the specified institution providing care

65歳以上（第1号被保険者）、40歳から64
歳までの医療保険の加入者（第2号被保険者）
の2区分があるが、実際のサービス対象者は
原則65歳以上。申請後の訪問調査と医師の
意見書をもとに審査・認定が行われ、サービ
ス利用時に所得に応じて1～3割を自己負担
する

Participants in the insurance scheme are
classified into first level (those older than 65),
and second level (those between 40 and 64).
But the only ones, in principle, to receive the
service are 65 or older. After an application
is made, an investigation and certification is
made based on a home visit and an opinion
from a doctor. Depending on their income,
the patient pays 10 to 30% themselves.

サービス例 Typical services
訪問介護・訪問入浴・訪問看護・デイケア・居宅療養管理指導・福祉用具支給など Home care, home bathing, home nursing, day care, home treatment advice, medical care equipment, etc.

□施行する implement

介護保障付き保険
Health insurance that includes home care

寝たきりや認知症で、要介護状態が一定期間続いている被保険者に支給される民間の保険

A private insurance under which the bedridden and those with senile dementia receive payment after the condition has continued for a certain period.

損害保険会社の保険 Insurance from property insurance companies	生命保険会社・農協の保険 Insurance provided by life insurance companies, and the agricultural cooperative
支払い限度額内で、医療費や介護機器購入費などの費用が支給される Payment made within maximum limits to cover medical expenses, care equipment expenses, and other costs.	保険料額に応じて、最高1000万円ぐらいまで支払われ、死亡時に一定の保険金が出るものもある Depending on the premium, a maximum of 10 million yen is paid out, along with a fixed payment upon death.

加入する際は、保険契約の内容を細部までチェックしておく必要がある。いざという時の給付条件は厳しく設定されている

When taking out insurance, it is important to check the details. The conditions for payment are often extremely difficult to meet.

Chapter 4
The Home

第4章 家庭

大事なことなのでじっくり読もう！
This Is Important! Read Carefully.

35

家庭（かてい）

　日本の戸籍制度は諸外国にくらべ閉鎖的と言われて久しい。その象徴が、「民法」に定める夫婦同姓の原則。戸籍は夫婦が単位となるが、これは夫を家長とする旧来の“家制度”の名残りという一面もある。

　戸籍は婚姻届で新たに作成されるが、この届出をしない夫婦の子は、戸籍のない子としてパスポートが発給されない、相続分が実子の半分、などの差別を受ける。法務大臣の諮問機関である法制審議会は1995年9月、“夫婦同姓を原則とするが、別姓も可、子の姓は夫婦どちらかと同一姓”との選択的夫婦別姓制度の導入を答申した。

□戸籍制度 family register system
□閉鎖的 restrictive
□民法 civil law
□同姓 same surname
□家長 head of the household

□名残り leftover
□諮問機関 inquiry body
□法制審議会 legal deliberative body
□答申する propose

Family Register System

Compared with other countries, the family register system in Japan has long been said to be restrictive. The most conspicuous example of this is the rule that married couples must have the same surnames, as decided under civil law. The family register makes the married couple the basic unit, but it can also be seen as a leftover from the old family system in which the husband was the head of the household.

A new family register is drawn up when a couple submits a notification of marriage. Children of couples who do not submit such notification have to face various forms of discrimination—for example, they will not be able to obtain passports, and they will only receive half the inheritance of children who have a family register. In September 1995, a legal deliberative body, an inquiry body of the Minister of Justice, proposed that a new system should be introduced whereby couples would in principle bear the same surname, but different names were possible, and their offspring could choose the name of one or the other of their parents.

家庭

婚姻届
Notification of marriage

→

新戸籍
A new register
is made

夫婦の一方が相手の戸籍に入籍するという
形で作成される

One or the other in the couple has a register
made in his or her name, and enters his or
her spouse's name into it.

◁))

戸籍の事務処理のコンピューター導入で、誤字は
自動的に訂正されるが、俗字は従来のまま使用し
てよいことになった

When people's names are entered into the records by
computer, mistakes in the characters receive automatic
correction; however nonstandard characters are allowed
to stand according to usage.

戸籍には氏名の読みがなが記載されていないが、
法改正で2024年度から全国民の読みがな登録
が始まる

Pronunciations of names have not historically been
recorded in the family register; however, following a
revision to the law, starting in 2024 the pronunciations of
all citizens' names will be recorded.

◁))

戸籍は夫の姓、仕事では旧姓を使う女性が増えている。子どもが生まれた時だけ入
籍して、再びペーパー離婚をするという荒ワザを使う人も。苗字が変わらないのを
恥としていた日本女性の結婚観は大きく変わった

Nowadays many women have started to use their husband's family name in the
family register, but their maiden name at the workplace. Also increasing is the
number of people who take out a family register only upon the birth of a child, after
which they then file notification of divorce. It is considered to be a source of shame
if a Japanese woman never changed her name; it now seems that such views have
undergone a huge change.

名前 なまえ Names	氏（姓）は夫婦同一が原則 し せい ふうふ どういつ げんそく In principle, couples share the same family name.
父母との続柄 ふ ぼ つづきがら Parental Lineage	嫡出子と非嫡出子の区別をする ちゃくしゅつ し ひ ちゃくしゅつ し く べつ Note is taken of whether the parties are legitimate or illegitimate offspring of their parents.
養親子 ようしんし Adoptions	実子と同様の特別養子以外は養子と記載 じっし どうよう とくべつようし いがい ようし き さい Children other than a couple's biological children and special adoptions considered to be of equal status are registered as adopted.

戸籍の主な記載事項

Main information entered into family register

◁))

戸籍には、婚姻届を出した正式な夫婦の子は「長男、二男…長女、二女…」と記載されるが、婚外子の場合は「男、女」とだけ記載される。なお、住民票に記載される世帯主と子の続柄は、嫡出子・非嫡出子（ただし認知が前提になる）の区別や長男・二男、養子などの区別なく、すべて「子」と統一される

In the registers, the children of couples who have submitted notification of marriage are noted as "eldest son," "second son," "eldest daughter." Illegitimate children are simply noted as "boy" or "girl." The details in the certificate of residence concerning the relationship of children to the head of each household were changed to make no differentiation between legitimate and illegitimate offspring. Further, offspring are noted simply as "child" regardless of whether they are eldest or youngest, biological or adopted.

◁))

婚姻届を出していない夫婦の間に生まれた子どもは、婚外子と呼ばれる
こんいんとどけ だ ふうふ あいだ う こ こんがいし よ

A child born to couples who have not submitted a notification of marriage is called an extramarital child.

□ 入籍する enroll in a registry
□ 俗字 nonstandard character
□ 旧姓 maiden name

□ 嫡出子 legitimate offspring
□ 非嫡出子 illegitimate offspring
□ 婚外子 illegitimate child

□ 住民票 certificate of residence
□ 世帯主 head of household

家_か庭_{てい}

戸籍原本と住民基本台帳
Original copies of the register and residents' ledger

届出
Notification

本籍地の市区町村役所
Village, Town, Ward or City Office of Place of Permanent Domicile

戸籍原本
Original Register

夫婦を単位にした記録

Record taken using the married couple as basic unit

戸籍謄(抄)本
(Abridged) transcripts of register

謄本は原本をすべて写した書面、抄本は一部を写した書面

A transcript is a complete copy of the original family register, whereas an extract is a partial copy.

戸籍原本に記録される届出
Details entered on Original Copy of Family Register

出生届	Notification of Births
入籍届	Notification of Entry into Family Registers
分籍届	Notification of Segregation from Family Register
転籍届	Notification of Transfer of Family Register
婚姻届	Notification of Marriage
名・氏の変更届	Notification of Change of Personal or Family Name
復氏届	Notification of Reversion to Original Family Name
(特別) 養子縁組届	Notification of (Special) Adoption
死亡届	Notification of Death

◁))

外国人が日本国籍を得る（帰化する）には、原則として継続して5年以上居住している、20歳以上、経済基盤がある等の条件を満たすことが必要

For a foreigner to gain Japanese citizenship (be naturalized), he or she must have lived five consecutive years in Japan, be twenty or older, and be financially sound, among other conditions.

住所地の市区町村役所（場）
Village, Town, Ward or City Office of Place of Residence

住民基本台帳
Residents' Ledger

世帯ごとの個人記録

Record is made of each individual in a household.

住民票
Resident Card

住民登録
Registration of Residence

住民基本台帳に記録される届出
Notifications registered on the Residents' Ledger

転居届	Notification of Change of Address
転入届	Notification of Moving In
転出届	Notification of Moving Out
世帯主変更届	Notification of Change of Head of Household
世帯変更届	Notification of Change of Household

◁)) 出生届・死亡届は、届出をすると自動的に住民基本台帳に記録されるしくみになっている

Notifications made in the family register of births and deaths are also automatically made on the residents' ledger.

36

結婚のしくみ

家庭

◁))　結婚は、**当事者同士**の意思で決まるものだが、法律上は**婚姻届**を提出することによって初めて正式な夫婦関係とされる。届出のないものは、**内縁関係**と呼ばれる。婚姻届は、当事者と証人が**所定用紙**に署名・押印して、市区町村の役所に提出すればよく、それが**受理**されれば成立する。ただし、男性は18歳以上、女性は16歳以上の年齢制限があるほか、**重婚**や**近親婚**は禁止されている。

　最近は、**再婚**というケースも多いが、女性の場合は離婚届を提出してから100日経たないと婚姻届は受理されない。また、離婚時に妊娠していないとの医師の証明書があれば、すぐ再婚できる。

□当事者同士　two parties involved
□婚姻届　Notification of Marriage
□内縁関係　common-law spouses
□所定用紙　prescribed form

□受理　acceptance
□重婚　polygamous marriage
□近親婚　marriage with close relatives
□再婚　remarriage

Marriage

Marriage is something that is decided upon by the two parties involved, but legally it is only when they submit a Notification of Marriage that a man and a women formally become husband and wife. Without this notification, even people who have gone through the ceremony are treated as "common-law" spouses. The Notification of Marriage is a form that has to be signed and stamped with the seal of both parties and a witness, and all they have to do is submit it at local government offices. With official acceptance, the marriage. Comes into being. Some restrictions apply: men have to be at least 18 years of age, and women 16; and polygamous marriages and marriages with close relatives are against the law.

In recent years, more and more people are going in for remarriage after divorce or a spouse's death. A woman has to wait at least 100 days after she has submitted Notification of Divorce before submitting a Notification of Marriage. Additionally, if a woman has a doctor's certificate declaring that she was not pregnant at the time of her divorce, she can remarry immediately.

家庭

結婚は、婚姻届の提出によって、法的に成立する

A marriage comes into being legally with the submission of a Notice of Marriage

届出
Submission

市区町村の役所

Appropriate government office at city, ward, town or village level

休日、夜間も受け付けてくれる

This is possible even on holidays and at night.

18歳未満の未成年者は、両親の結婚同意書が必要

People who are under 18 years of age, the official age of adulthood, have to obtain written consent to the marriage from both sets of parents.

Written Consent

国際結婚のしくみ

　日本人が外国人と結婚する場合は、日本人は日本の法律、外国人はその国の法律に従うことが原則。婚姻の届出は、結婚する国の法律にもとづいて行う。

　外国人の場合、その国の駐在政府機関が発行する婚姻証明書が必要になる。

　日本人が外国人と結婚しても、新しい戸籍はつくられない。外国人も帰化しない限り、日本の戸籍には入れない。ただし、生まれた子供はいずれかの国籍が選べる。

□同意書　written consent
□駐在する　be stationed in

□不受理申立書　petition of non-acceptance

🔊))

本人にその意思がないのに、まれに親などが一方的に
婚姻手続きを進めてしまうケースがある。そんな場
合は、事前に婚姻届**不受理申立書**を提出しておくと、
6か月間は受理しないことになっている

There are very rare cases in which parents attempt
to register a marriage even though one or both the
parties in question have no intention of marrying.
In such cases, if the unwilling party (or parties)
submit in advance a petition of non-acceptance,
the marriage registration will not be recognized for a
period of six months.

Marriage between Japanese and non-Japanese people

When a Japanese person marries a non-Japanese person, the general rule is that the Japanese must abide by Japanese law, and the non-Japanese must abide by the law of his or her country. Notice of marriage should be carried out in accordance with the laws of the country in which marriage takes place.

The non-Japanese person must fill in the forms for Certificate of Marriage available at the representative organ of his country's government stationed in Japan.

In the case of marriages between Japanese and non-Japanese, certain procedures have to be taken before the couple take out a new family register: the non-Japanese person has to become a naturalized Japanese citizen to be able to enter his or her name in a family register in Japan. The offspring born to the couple, however, can choose which nationality of their parents they would prefer.

37

家庭
か
てい

◁)) "成田離婚"や"関空離婚"という言葉がある。結婚式を挙げ、海外への新
婚旅行からの**帰途**で、もう夫婦喧嘩。空港で別れたまま離婚というケース
である。

　もっとも、夫婦の合意があればその理由にかかわらず、離婚届を役所に
提出すれば離婚は成立する。だが、この"夫婦の合意"というのが問題で、
結婚は**たやすく**離婚は難しいとされる**ゆえん**である。離婚を前提とする当
事者間での話し合いで結論が出ない場合は、家庭裁判所に**調停**を依頼する。
この場合も、夫婦の一方が反対ならば、離婚はできない。それでも強引に
離婚を進めようとする場合、地方裁判所へ**提訴する**が、相当の理由がなけ
れば請求を**棄却**されてしまう。

□帰途 return

□たやすく be easy

□ゆえん reason

□調停 arbitration

□提訴する file a lawsuit

□棄却される be dismissed

Divorce

"Narita Airport divorce" and "Kansai Airport divorce" have become well-known expressions. After the wedding, a couple goes abroad all smiles for the honeymoon trip, but when they return they refuse to speak to each other. There are even cases where they split up immediately at the airport and then get a divorce.

If both parties are agreed, a marriage is dissolved regardless of the reasons, providing a Notification of Divorce is filed with the appropriate government office. However, this mutual agreement is precisely the difficulty—and one reason behind the saying that "Marriages might be easy, but divorces are hard." In cases where both parties want a divorce but are unable to come to an agreement on the terms, they request arbitration from the family court. Even with such recourse, one party may still refuse to agree to the divorce, which will make it impossible. If the other party is still determined and refuses to give up, the matter goes to the district court. However, there then has to be an overwhelming and undeniable reason for a decision to be approved.

家庭

協議離婚
Consensual divcorce

離婚届

Notification of
Divorce

**夫婦の合意が
あればよい**

All that is needed is
the consent of the
couple.

届出
Submission

市区町村の役所
Appropriate government office at city, ward, town or village level

◁)) 離婚の意思がないのに離婚届を一方的に出されそうになった場合は市区町村の役所に「離婚届不受理申出」を行う

If one spouse suspects that his or her partner is going to go expressly against his or her own wishes and to unilaterally issue a Notification of Divorce, it is possible to file a Petition for Non-acceptance of the Notice of Divorce.

夫婦の一方が同意しない場合
When one party of the marriage refuses to consent to divorce

調停申立
Petition for Arbitration

相手の居住地のある家庭裁判所へ調停を依頼する

The person seeking the divorce requests arbitration at the family court in the area of domicile of his or her spouse.

"I hate to think about how much compensation I'll have to pay!"

慰謝料が心配だ……!!

家庭裁判所
Family Court

裁判ではなく、調停委員を交えた話し合い

The proceedings do not actually take the form of a court case, but rather discussions with members of an arbitration committee.

不成立
Divorce not approved

地方裁判所
District Court

Court Case
裁判

費用と時間がかかる

This involves considerable time and money.

成立
Divorce approved

判決
Judgment

調停離婚
Arbitrated Divorce

裁判離婚
Adjudicated Divorce

法事のしくみ

法事は死者の霊をとむらう儀式である。大別すると仏式、神式、キリスト教式の3種があるが、わが国では仏式が最もなじみが深い。そこで、仏式を例にとって法事のプロセスを見てみると、**忌明けの法要**である四十九日法要までは七日毎に、それ以後は毎月の**命日**に霊をなぐさめるというしきたりになっている。これは、**故人**の霊が安らかにあの世に旅立てるようにする**遺族**のつとめで、その大きな区切りが一年後の祥月命日にとり行われる一周忌法要である。以後の法要は次第に間隔が長くなり、五十回忌をもって完了するのが慣例である。

□ とむらう pay respect to
□ 忌明け end of mourning
□ 法要 Buddhist memorial service

□ 命日 obit
□ 故人 the deceased
□ 遺族 bereaved family

Memorial Service

Memorial services are held to pay respect to the spirit of the deceased. The three main categories are Buddhist, Shinto, and Christian services, Buddhist services being the most common in Japan. In Buddhism, the mourning period lasts for 49 days, with ceremonies held by the family on every seventh day during that period, and then once a month on the obit. It is the responsibility of the family to carry out these rites to help the deceased proceed to the other world. A memorial service is held on the first anniversary after passing, called the *shōtsuki-meinichi*. After the first year, the length of time between rites gradually increases. It is not uncommon for the extended mourning period to end on the 50th anniversary of death.

家庭（かてい）

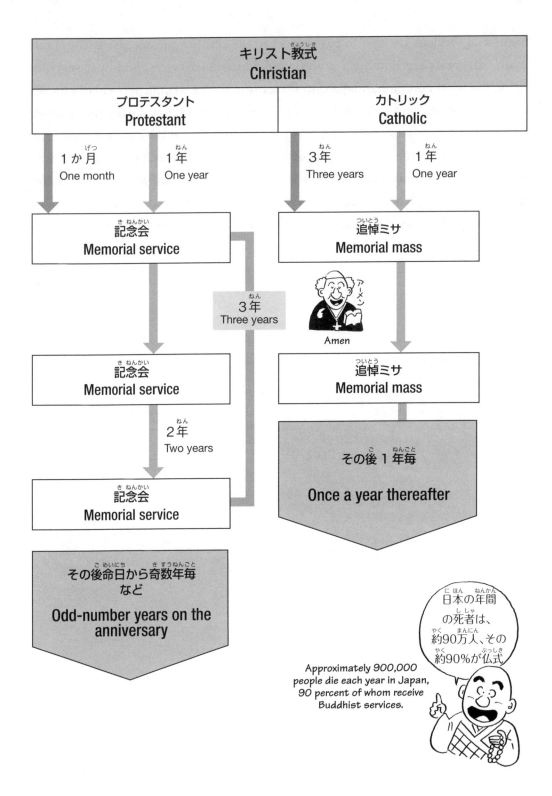

キリスト教式（きょうしき）
Christian

プロテスタント **Protestant**	カトリック **Catholic**

1か月（げつ）
One month

1年（ねん）
One year

3年（ねん）
Three years

1年（ねん）
One year

記念会（きねんかい）
Memorial service

追悼ミサ（ついとう）
Memorial mass

3年（ねん）
Three years

Amen

記念会（きねんかい）
Memorial service

追悼ミサ（ついとう）
Memorial mass

2年（ねん）
Two years

記念会（きねんかい）
Memorial service

その後（ご）1年毎（ねんごと）

Once a year thereafter

その後命日（ごめいにち）から奇数年毎（きすうねんごと）
など

Odd-number years on the anniversary

日本（に ほん）の年間（ねんかん）の死者（ししゃ）は、約（やく）90万人（まんにん）、その約（やく）90％が仏式（ぶっしき）

Approximately 900,000 people die each year in Japan, 90 percent of whom receive Buddhist services.

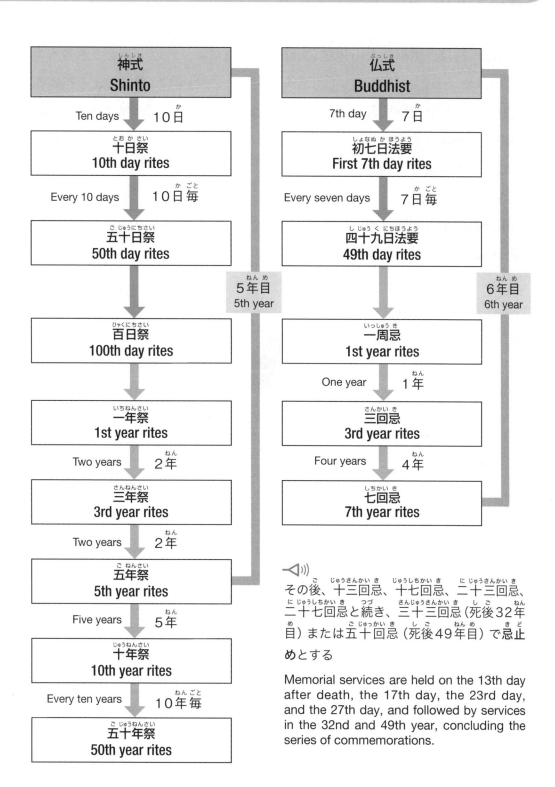

神式 (しんしき) Shinto	仏式 (ぶっしき) Buddhist
Ten days 10日 (か)	7th day 7日 (か)
十日祭 (とおかさい) 10th day rites	初七日法要 (しょなのかほうよう) First 7th day rites
Every 10 days 10日毎 (かごと)	Every seven days 7日毎 (かごと)
五十日祭 (ごじゅうにちさい) 50th day rites	四十九日法要 (しじゅうくにちほうよう) 49th day rites

5年目 (ねんめ) 5th year
6年目 (ねんめ) 6th year

百日祭 (ひゃくにちさい) 100th day rites	一周忌 (いっしゅうき) 1st year rites
	One year 1年 (ねん)
一年祭 (いちねんさい) 1st year rites	三回忌 (さんかいき) 3rd year rites
Two years 2年 (ねん)	Four years 4年 (ねん)
三年祭 (さんねんさい) 3rd year rites	七回忌 (しちかいき) 7th year rites
Two years 2年 (ねん)	
五年祭 (ごねんさい) 5th year rites	
Five years 5年 (ねん)	
十年祭 (じゅうねんさい) 10th year rites	
Every ten years 10年毎 (ねんごと)	
五十年祭 (ごじゅうねんさい) 50th year rites	

🔊))
その後、十三回忌 (じゅうさんかいき)、十七回忌 (じゅうしちかいき)、二十三回忌 (にじゅうさんかいき)、二十七回忌 (にじゅうしちかいき)と続 (つづ)き、三十三回忌 (さんじゅうさんかいき) (死後 (しご)32年目 (ねんめ))または五十回忌 (ごじゅっかいき) (死後 (しご)49年目 (ねんめ))で忌止 (きど)めとする

Memorial services are held on the 13th day after death, the 17th day, the 23rd day, and the 27th day, and followed by services in the 32nd and 49th year, concluding the series of commemorations.

□忌止め concluding the series of commemorations

39

遺産相続のしくみ

家庭

🔊 遺産相続は、**被相続人**の死亡（**失踪宣言制度**により死亡とみなされるものも含む）によって、開始される。遺産の相続分については**遺言**による**指定相続分**と、それがない場合の**法定相続分**とがある。さらに遺言がない場合は、相続人の協議・合意による分割も可能だ。遺産とはいえ、なかには借金などのマイナス財産が含まれているケースもある。その場合は、相続を**放棄**することもできる。

　相続税の申告期間は原則として10か月間となっているので、この間に相続分の確定と納税が必要だ。

□ 被相続人 inherited
□ 失踪宣言制度 be declared by law to have "absconded" or "disappeared"
□ 遺言 a will

□ 指定相続分 designated inheritance share
□ 法定相続分 statutory inheritance share
□ 放棄する abandon
□ 相続税 inheritance tax

Property Inheritance

Property inheritance commences on the death of the person from whom property is to be inherited (and this includes cases where a person is declared by law to have "absconded" or "disappeared"). Inheritance covers both those sections of a person's property laid down in a will, and parts for which no will has been drawn up, in which case the apportionment is decided in accordance with provisions in the law. In cases where there is no will at all, property division is carried out through division based on discussions and agreement of inheritors. Of course, it is often the case that debts are inherited by the individuals who inherit property and estate. In this case, the inheritors may choose to abandon their inheritance.

The period allowed in which one has to submit a report for tax purposes is 10 months; during this time one should both file a final tax report and pay the requisite taxes.

家庭

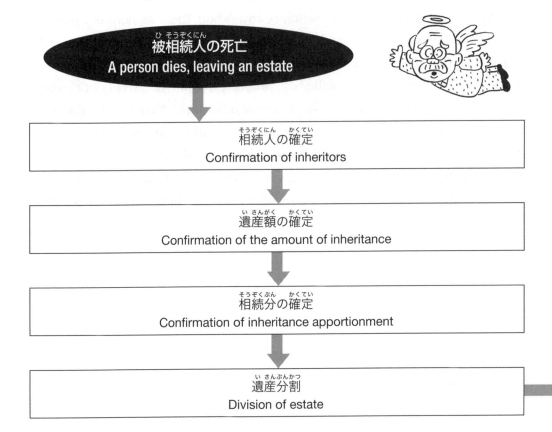

被相続人の死亡
A person dies, leaving an estate

相続人の確定
Confirmation of inheritors

遺産額の確定
Confirmation of the amount of inheritance

相続分の確定
Confirmation of inheritance apportionment

遺産分割
Division of estate

相続税の**基礎控除**は、定額控除3000万円、相続人1人当たりの比例控除は600万円

The basic rate of deduction for inheritance tax involves a fixed deduction of 30 million yen, and then 0.6 million yen for every inheritor.

配偶者に対しては、法定相続分または1億6000万円までは非課税

For spouses of the deceased, however, tax exemption applies to the legally recognized inheritance, or up to 160 million yen.

□基礎控除 basic rate of deduction
□相続の開始 commencement of inheritance
□申し立てる submit a petition

The Home

借金を相続しなければならないときは、相続放棄ができる。その場合は、相続の開始を知った日から3か月以内に家庭裁判所へ申し立てる

It is possible to abandon one's inheritance to avoid inheriting a person's debts. In such cases, one submits a petition to the family court within three months of the commencement of inheritance.

死亡の日の翌日から原則として10か月以内に行うこと

Obligatory within 10 months from the day after the inheritee's decease.

相続税申告・納税

Inheritance tax
return and payment

税務署

Tax Office

納税は一時払いが原則ですが、分割払いや物納の救済措置もあります

"In principle, inheritance tax should be paid in one lump sum, but remedial measures are available that enable payment in installments, as well as payment in kind."

確定申告のしくみ

40

家庭

◁)) 　個人の所得にかかる所得税は毎年、前年1年分の所得を総合して税額を計算し、申告納付することになっている。収入が会社からの給料・賞与のみという人については、支給されたときに源泉徴収されている税額を、年間を通じて再計算する年末調整で納税手続きは完了する。ただし年収が2000万円を超えた人、不動産などを売却して所得があった人はサラリーマンでも確定申告が必要。ローンで住宅を購入したり、年間10万円を超える医療費を支払った人は、還付申告すれば税金の払い戻しを受けられる。

□ 所得　income
□ 所得税　income tax
□ 申告納付　self-assessment and payment of tax
□ 源泉徴収　tax withheld, withholding tax at source

□ 年末調整　year-end adjustment
□ 納税手続き　tax payment procedure
□ 確定申告　income tax return
□ 還付申告する　file a refund claim

Filing an Income Tax Return

Self-assessment and payment of tax on individual income are calculated based on the total income of the previous year. The payment procedure ends with year-end adjustments for tax withheld from paychecks over the course of the year for people whose income only involves salaries and bonuses from companies. However, those who make over 20 million yen a year and those with income from the sale of real estate must file an income tax return even if they are salaried employees. Individuals who have taken out loans to buy homes or have paid medical expenses over 100,000 yen a year can get a refund on their taxes if they file a return.

家庭

所得税の確定申告
Filing an income tax return

給与所得（給与・賞与） Earned income (salary/bonuses)	利子・配当・不動産・事業・譲渡・一時・雑などの各所得 Income from interest, dividends, real estate, business, inheritance, etc., or occasional, miscellaneous, etc., income

年末調整 End of year adjustments	源泉徴収 Withholding tax at source	源泉徴収 Withholding tax at source

簡易給与所得表、速算表 Simplified compensation statement	必要経費・譲渡の特別控除など Special deduction for necessary expenses and inheritance

所得金額
Income tax amount

所得控除
Income tax deductions

社会保険料・生命保険料・損害保険料・医療費・寄付金控除、配偶者・扶養などの人的控除および基礎控除

Personal and basic deductions such as social insurance premiums, life insurance premiums, health insurance premiums, medical expenses, charitable deductions, spouse, and dependents

The Home

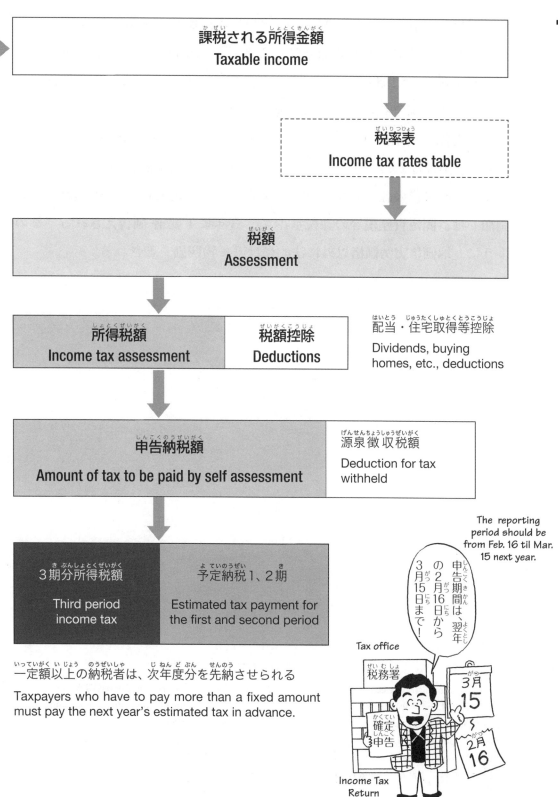

課税(かぜい)される所得金額(しょとくきんがく)
Taxable income

税率表(ぜいりつひょう)
Income tax rates table

税額(ぜいがく)
Assessment

所得税額(しょとくぜいがく)
Income tax assessment

税額控除(ぜいがくこうじょ)
Deductions

配当(はいとう)・住宅取得等控除(じゅうたくしゅとくとうこうじょ)
Dividends, buying homes, etc., deductions

申告納税額(しんこくのうぜいがく)
Amount of tax to be paid by self assessment

源泉徴収税額(げんせんちょうしゅうぜいがく)
Deduction for tax withheld

3期分所得税額(きぶんしょとくぜいがく)
Third period income tax

予定納税1、2期(よていのうぜい)
Estimated tax payment for the first and second period

The reporting period should be from Feb. 16 til Mar. 15 next year.

申告期間(しんこくきかん)は、翌年(よくとし)の2月(がつ)16日(にち)から3月(がつ)15日(にち)まで！

Tax office

税務署(ぜいむしょ)

確定申告(かくていしんこく)

3月(がつ)15

2月(がつ)16

Income Tax Return

一定額以上(いっていがくいじょう)の納税者(のうぜいしゃ)は、次年度分(じねんどぶん)を先納(せんのう)させられる

Taxpayers who have to pay more than a fixed amount must pay the next year's estimated tax in advance.

185

地価のしくみ

41

家庭

　地価には取引上の「**実務価格**」と、法律でその基準を定めたものとがある。地価の基準となるのは**地価公示法**による「**公示価格**」で、国土交通省が毎年1月1日現在で調査し、4月1日付で発表。自治体による**指導価格**の目安とされる地価である。次に、**規制区域**内の基準価格の凍結や取引許可制を定めた**国土利用計画法**にもとづく地価を、俗に「**基準地価格**」という。さらに、**国税庁**が毎年7月1日現在で調査する「**路線価**」がある。これは、相続税や贈与税の課税基準になるものだ。一方、**地方税**の「**固定資産税評価額**」は、**固定資産税**等の課税基準で、3年に1度**評価替えされる**。このように、地価は**実勢価格**以外に法的には「**一物四価**」とされる。

- □実務価格　administrative cost
- □地価公示法　Land Price Disclosure Act
- □公示価格　standard land price
- □指導価格　guideline price
- □規制区域　regulated district
- □国土利用計画法　National Land Utilization Planning Act
- □基準地価格　regulated land price
- □国税庁　the Bureau of Internal Revenue
- □路線価　value of land facing a thoroughfare
- □地方税　regional tax
- □固定資産税評価額　assessed value of fixed assets
- □固定資産税　tax base for fixed assets
- □評価替えされる　be re-evaluated
- □実勢価格　administrative cost
- □一物四価　four prices for one item

Land Prices

The price of land involves the "administrative costs" of doing business, and land price standards as prescribed by law. The standard land price is made public by the Land Price Disclosure Act. The Ministry of Land, Infrastructure and Transport carries out a survey every year on January 1, and announces the results on April 1. The land prices are a rough standard of guideline prices by municipality. In addition to this are prices based on the National Land Utilization Planning Act that establish the standard linkage and dealing prices within regulated districts. These are popularly called, "regulated land prices." The Bureau of Internal Revenue also conducts a survey every year on July 1 to appraise the value of land facing a thoroughfare. This appraisal becomes the tax base for inheritance and gift taxes. On the other hand, the "assessed value of fixed assets," is a tax base for fixed assets in regional taxes, and is re-evaluated every three years. In this way, there are "four prices for one item" in addition to the administrative cost when dealing with the price of land.

公示価格
Posted price

"I think this one's worth about this much."

私達はこれを基準にしています

"We'll make this the standard."

この場所はこれぐらいの価格だな！

公的機関

Public Agency

国土交通省

Ministry of Land, Infrastructure and Transport

1㎡あたりの値段

Price per square meter

実勢価格を100として、70〜80％くらい

70 to 80 percent of administrative costs

基準地価格
Standard land price

ちょっと安いんじゃないの!?

"Don't you think that's a little cheap?"

Price regulation

しかし法律で価格が決められているんです

"The price is prescribed by law."

価格規定

地主

Property owner

公示価格と同じくらいの比率

About the same rate as the posted price

路線価
Value of land facing a thoroughfare

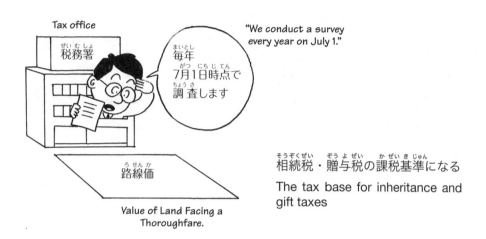

Tax office
税務署

毎年
7月1日時点で
調査します

"We conduct a survey every year on July 1."

路線価

Value of Land Facing a Thoroughfare.

相続税・贈与税の課税基準になる

The tax base for inheritance and gift taxes

固定資産税評価額
Assessed value of fixed assets

固定資産課税台帳
Fixed Property
Tax Ledger

固定資産税評価額の
1.4%

Fixed Property Tax
(1.4 percent of the appraised value)

3年に1度、評価替えが行われる

Re-evaluated once every three years.

ゴミ処理のしくみ

42

家庭

🔊))　文明はその裏側に、ゴミという難題を抱えこんできた。すでに大都市部では、処分しきれないゴミが山積している状態で、いずれ処分地をめぐってゴミ戦争が勃発するという物騒な予言もあるほどだ。

　消費経済のメッカ・東京では、1日約1万トンを超えるゴミが回収され、**廃棄物処理施設**や**埋立地**で処分しているが、ゴミの増えるスピードに処理能力が追いつかないのが現状。燃えるゴミ、燃えないゴミの**分別収集**は今や常識化しているし、**粗大ゴミ**の引取りの有料化も進んでいる。ゴミとして放置されることが多かった家電製品も、販売店に**引取り業務(有料)**が課せられるようになった。都市部の自治体では、一般ゴミの有料回収が進んでいる。

□難題　extremely difficult problem

□山積する　accumulate

□消費経済　consumerism

□廃棄物処理施設　waste disposable center

□埋立地　dumping ground

□分別収集　separate collection (of garbage)

□粗大ゴミ　large items of refuse

□引取る　take back

Waste Disposal

Our modern lifestyle of convenience and consumerism has brought as its downside the extremely difficult problem of garbage. Already in large cities and towns, the mountains of refuse accumulated are more than can be dealt with, and predictions have even been made that local areas will soon be having "trash wars" with each other over places reserved to dump waste.

In Tokyo, which is the Mecca of consumerism, every day more than 10,000 tons of refuse are collected. At the moment they are dealt with at waste disposal centers and dumping grounds, but it's a sad fact that the amount of trash is increasing at such a rate that they can't really keep up with it. Nowadays, it goes without saying that waste collection is carried out separately for burnable waste and non-burnable waste, and it's also common to arrange for special services to come and collect large items of refuse (such as furniture or refrigerators) for a fee. In previous times, electrical goods often used to be thrown out with the other trash, but nowadays distributors are obliged, for a fee, to take them back. More municipalities in urban areas are now charging for the collection of general garbage.

家庭(かてい)

燃(も)えるゴミ
Burnable waste

家庭(かてい)から出(だ)される一般廃棄物(いっぱんはいきぶつ)は年間(ねんかん)4000万(まん)トン超(ちょう)。ゴミの分別(ぶんべつ)とリサイクルは21世紀(せいき)の重要課題(じゅうようかだい)だ

The waste produced by ordinary households exceeds 40,000,000 tons a year. The separation and recycling of garbage is a serious problem for the 21st century.

粗大(そだい)ゴミ
Large items of refuse

破砕処理施設(はさいしょりしせつ)
Crushing apparatus

粗大(そだい)ゴミは機械(きかい)で小(ちい)さく砕(くだ)き、容積(ようせき)を減(へ)らす

A machine crushes the large items into small pieces, to take up less space.

燃(も)えないゴミ
Non-burnable waste

陸路(りくろ)で
By road

船(ふね)で
By sea

□一般廃棄物 general waste

◁))

ゴミの焼却熱を発電に利用する廃棄物処理場が増えてきた。さらに発電後の蒸気を用いて温水プールなどへの熱供給を行うケースもある

More and more waste disposal sites are using the heat produced by waste disposal for the generation of electricity. There are also more instances of heated swimming pools being heated by the steam so generated.

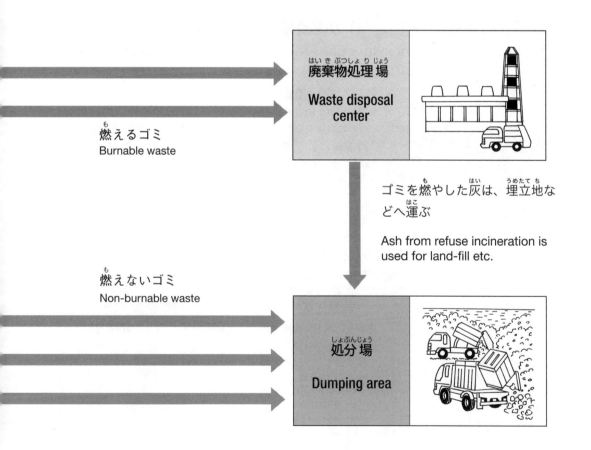

廃棄物処理場
Waste disposal center

燃えるゴミ
Burnable waste

ゴミを燃やした灰は、埋立地などへ運ぶ

Ash from refuse incineration is used for land-fill etc.

燃えないゴミ
Non-burnable waste

処分場
Dumping area

公道を走行する自動車の安全性能や環境保全をチェックするために義務付けられているのが、自動車検査(車検)登録である。これには、ディーラーや整備業者に任せる整備車検、専門業者に任せる車検代行、所有者が自ら行うユーザー車検があり、通常は整備車検を利用するケースが多い。車種や用途によって検査期間が定められている(継続検査)。検査に合格すると、自動車検査証(車検証)と検査標章(ステッカー)が交付され、標章は自動車(フロントガラス)に貼付しなければならない。違反車には罰則規定がある。また、自動車の不具合を見つけるための法定点検(整備を含む)も義務付けられているが、24か月点検は車検と同時に受けることが多い。

家庭

自家用車(普通車・軽自動車)の継続検査と法定点検
Ongoing and statutory inspections for private vehicles (cars and K-cars)

継続検査 Ongoing inspections	
中古車の場合は、2年ごとに車検を受ける Used cars must be inspected every two years.	新車の場合は、購入後3年目に車検を受ける New cars must be inspected from the third year after purchase.

法定点検(12か月点検・24か月点検) Statutory inspection (12-month/24-month inspection)		
ユーザー Owner	認証工場 Certified garage	指定整備工場 Certified maintenance garage
点検 inspection ▼ 整備 Maintenance	点検 inspection ▼ 整備 Maintenance	点検 inspection ▼ 整備 Maintenance ▼ 完成検査 Completion inspection

Automobile Safety Inspection

Automobiles that drive on public roads must be checked for safety and environmental compliance under the Motor Vehicle Inspection and Registration System, popularly known as *shaken*. Inspection and maintenance may be left in the hands of a car dealer or maintenance garage, entrusted to an agent, or carried out by the owner, but the first option is the most popular. Ongoing inspections are carried out at regular intervals determined by vehicle type and purpose. Once a vehicle passes inspection, a vehicle inspection certificate and sticker are issued, and the sticker must be attached to the vehicle's windscreen. There are penal provisions for drivers of vehicles that do not meet these requirements. Statutory inspections (including maintenance) to identify faults in vehicles are also required, but most people have these 24-month inspections performed along with their *shaken* inspections.

Inspection station · cheap, quick, safe · 車検 · 安い 早い 安心

ユーザー車検を格安で代行する業者が急増している。だが、安かろう危なかろうでは困る

The number of businesses offering inspection services at rock-bottom prices is increasing rapidly. However, safety is one thing you don't want to treat lightly.

ユーザーが点検・整備をやり直して国の車検場に持ち込むか、指定整備工場で整備・検査を受ける

Owners may re-inspect and repair their own cars and then take them to a government inspection station or have the cars inspected and repaired by a certified garage.

書面検査
Paper inspection

不合格になった場合
When inspection is not passed

国の車検場
Government inspection station

- □ 公道 public road
- □ 環境保全 environmental compliance
- □ 自動車検査登録 Motor Vehicle Inspection and Registration System
- □ 整備業者 maintenance garage
- □ 整備車検 maintenance inspection
- □ 車検代行 vehicle inspection service
- □ ユーザー車検 user inspection
- □ 継続検査 continuous inspection
- □ 自動車検査証 vehicle inspection certificate
- □ 検査標章 inspection sticker
- □ 貼付する attach
- □ 罰則規定 penal provision
- □ 法定点検 statutory inspection

Chapter 5
Culture and Arts

第5章 文化・技芸

ゆったり気分で楽しもう！
Sit Back and Enjoy It!

44

文化財指定のしくみ

文化・技芸

◁)) 長い歴史を経た建物は私達に安らぎを与えてくれる。こうした歴史的文化財のうち、重要なものは文化財保護審議会の答申を経て、文化庁長官が重要文化財等の指定をする。建物や工芸品は重要文化財に、世界文化の観点からも重要なものは国宝に、音楽や技術は重要無形文化財に、衣服や家屋は重要有形民俗文化財に、城址等は史跡、庭園等は名勝、動物等は天然記念物に指定。これら文化財の管理者は保存行為に当たっては届け出や許可が必要。また、保存のための国庫補助も行われる。

□長い歴史を経た survived through the ages
□文化財保護審議会 Advisory Council on the Protection of Cultural Properties
□文化庁長官 Commissioner for Cultural Affairs
□重要文化財 Important Cultural Properties
□工芸品 folk craft
□国宝 National Treasure

□重要無形文化財 Important Intangible Cultural Property
□重要有形民俗文化財 Important Tangible Folk Cultural Property
□城址 ruin of castle
□史跡 Historical Site
□名勝 Place of Scenic Beauty
□天然記念物 Natural Monument

The Designation of Cultural Properties

Buildings and other monuments that have survived through the ages give us a sense of serenity and peace of mind. Commissioner for Cultural Affairs designates the most important of these historical sites as Important Cultural Properties, based upon reports from the Advisory Council on the Protection of Cultural Properties. Buildings and folk crafts are designated as Important Cultural Properties, with those deemed important from a global perspective declared National Treasures. Within these categories, music and traditional techniques of artisanship are called Important Intangible Cultural Properties. Clothing and houses come into the category of Important Tangible Cultural Properties or in some cases Folk Cultural Properties. Ruins of castles are declared Historical Sites, gardens and parks Places of Scenic Beauty, and plants, animals, and other natural phenomena as Natural Monuments. Those in charge of maintaining such cultural properties must apply for permission before performing any kind of preservation or restoration work. Government subsidies are made available for such purposes.

Culture and Arts

文化・技芸

周辺も含め、文化財の発見のため調査します

With the discovery of a cultural property, a survey, including the surrounding area, is conducted.

文化庁調査官

Agency for Cultural Affairs Survey Officer

↓

保護審議会

The Advisory Council on the Protection of Cultural Properties

↓

答申

Report

↓

文化庁長官

Commissioner for Cultural Affairs

• 文献等からも情報を得る

Information is also collected from written sources.

• 都道府県指定重要文化財も対象に

The survey also examines cultural properties designated as such by individual prefectures.

重要文化財等指定

Designation as Important Cultural Property

管理等のための国庫補助

Subsidies from the National Treasury for maintenance, etc.

文化庁長官の許可なく輸出すると……

If any of these are transported out of the country without the permission of the Commissioner for Cultural Affairs…

5年以下の懲役か禁固 または50万円以下の罰金

The responsible party shall be sentenced to a prison term of up to 5 years, or a fine of up to 500,000 yen.

Culture and Arts

重要文化財
Important Cultural Properties

国宝
National Treasures

重要無形文化財
Important Intangible
Cultural Properties

重要有形・無形民俗文化財
Important Tangible and Intangible
Folk Cultural Properties

史跡
Historical Sites

特別史跡
Special Historical Sites

名勝
Places of Scenic Beauty

特別名勝
Special Places of Scenic Beauty

天然記念物
National Monuments

特別天然記念物
Special National Monuments

こわしたりすると……

If any of these are damaged…

5年以下の懲役か禁固
または20万円以下の罰金

The responsible party shall be sentenced to
a prison term of up to 5 years, or a fine of
up to 200,000 yen.

45

◁))) 歌舞伎役者は原則的に世襲制である。原則的に、というのは役者の家に生まれなくとも、その道に入ることはできるからだ。23歳未満で役者を志す人は、国立劇場の歌舞伎俳優研修生試験のコースがある。合格すると２年間の基礎課程を経て、修了後は現役の役者のところに入門し、大部屋生活からスタートする。だが、研修生出身者の出世は望めず、親の七光り組がチャンスに恵まれるというのが梨園の伝統でもある。

　特に、次の見開きページのような大名跡は父子相伝で、最も格式が高い。なかでも市川家は、歌舞伎界の宗家として位置付けられてきた。そして、格式こそが日本古来の芸能にとって伝統を保持する手段なのだ。

□世襲制 hereditary succession
□〜の道に入る enter the career of
□国立劇場 National Theater
□修了後は upon completion
□大部屋生活 all share one, large, communal dressing room families
□親の七光り the offspring of the most illustrious

□梨園 world of the theater
□大名跡 famous family name
□父子相伝 passed on from father to son
□宗家 head family
□格式 rank
□保持する preserve

The Kabuki World

One becomes a kabuki actor generally only through hereditary succession. We say generally because even if one is not born into a kabuki family, it is still possible to take up training to become a kabuki actor. There is a special course of Kabuki Actor Training and Apprenticeship available at the National Theater for people under 23 years of age who decide that this is the career for them. If they are accepted, they study the basics for two years, and upon completion become the disciple of a professional kabuki actor, and make their start as actors who play less important roles (and all share one, large, communal dressing room). However, such actors can't hope to become great kabuki stars, for it is still very much the tradition of this world of the theater for only a very select few, the offspring of the most illustrious families, to be given opportunities.

As seen on the next pages, the famous family names passed on from father to son carry the most elevated social standing. The Ichikawa family, in particular, has been positioned as the head family of the kabuki world. And rank itself is the means of preserving tradition in the ancient Japanese performing arts.

文化・技芸

主な襲名のプロセス
How kabuki actors succeed to their names

Ichikawa Danjūrō 市川団十郎	Nakamura Utaemon 中村歌右衛門

2022年11月、第13代（白猿）が襲名。
屋号は成田屋

As of November 2022, Ichikawa Danjūro is Ichikawa Danjūro XIII. His acting house name is Narita-ya.

女形の大名跡で、現在は第7代。
屋号は成駒屋

Famous for playing female roles, the current Nakamura Utaemon is Nakamura Utaemon VII. His acting house name is Narikoma-ya.

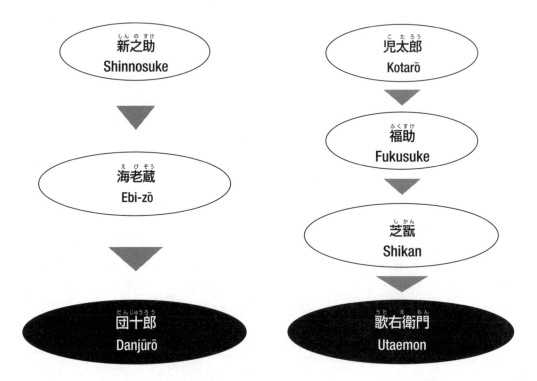

Matsumoto Kōshirō
松本幸四郎

現在は第10代。屋号は高麗屋

The present Matsumoto Kōshirō is Matsumoto Kōshirō X. His stage name is Kōrai-ya.

Onoe Kikugorō
尾上菊五郎

現在は第7代。屋号は音羽屋

The present Onoe Kikugorō is Onoe Kikugorō VII. His acting house name is Otowa-ya.

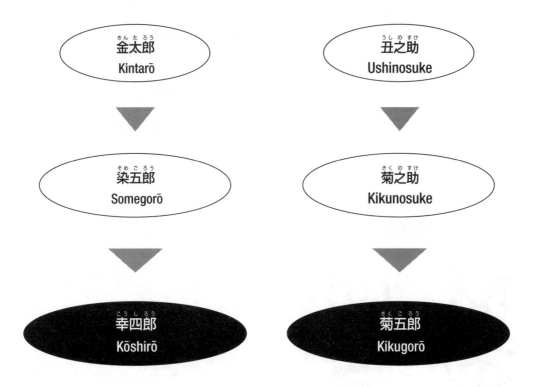

金太郎
Kintarō

染五郎
Somegorō

幸四郎
Kōshirō

丑之助
Ushinosuke

菊之助
Kikunosuke

菊五郎
Kikugorō

文化・技芸

歌舞伎舞台のしくみ
Tricks of the kabuki stage

◁))） 円の部分が廻り舞台で、電動で回転する。直径は約18m

Sometimes the stage has a round section that revolves, powered by electricity. The diameter of this section is 18 meters.

◁))） 舞台の大ぜりは建物など、小ぜりは人物、花道のすっぽんは妖怪などがせり上がって登場するしかけ

The large and small *seri* in the floor are contraptions (lifts, really) that allow objects and people to appear on stage—in the case of the large *seri*, stage props such as buildings, and in the case of the small *seri*, people. The *suppon* (literally, "snapping turtle") in the *hanamichi* (raised dais coming through the audience on which actors may make exits or entries) is a trapdoor that allows ghosts and the like to suddenly loom up onto the *hanamichi*, seemingly out of nowhere.

黒御簾

Black curtain (the musicians who provide accompaniment sit behind this.)

花道
Hanamichi

客席
Audience seats

揚幕
Curtain (through which actors make their entry and exit)

くまどり
Kumadori

善人
goody

悪人
villain

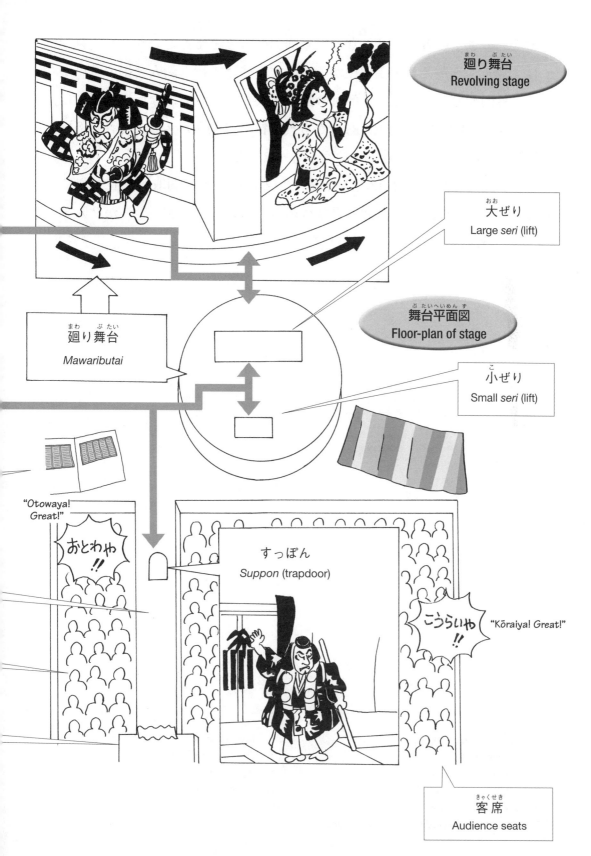

廻り舞台
Revolving stage

大ぜり
Large *seri* (lift)

舞台平面図
Floor-plan of stage

廻り舞台
Mawaributai

小ぜり
Small *seri* (lift)

"Otowaya! Great!"

おとわや‼

すっぽん
Suppon (trapdoor)

こうらいや‼

"Kōraiya! Great!"

客席
Audience seats

46

大相撲のしくみ

文化・技芸

力士をめざす若者たちは、なんと年間100人を超えるという。この背景には、50近くを数える**相撲部屋**がその**興亡**を賭けて行う**新人発掘**の戦いがある。外国人力士の増加も、**部屋の乱立**と決して**無縁ではない**。部屋には力士の**ランクに応じて**、**相撲協会**から**養成費**や**奨励金**が入る。それが部屋の経営をうるおす**財源**になるというしくみなのだ。

現在、力士総数は約700人といわれている。このうち**関取**へ出世できるのは1割程度、最高位の横綱へ昇りつめられるのはせいぜい1人か2人という厳しい世界である。

- □ 相撲部屋　sumo wrestling stable
- □ 興亡　existence
- □ 新人発掘　new talent discovery
- □ 部屋の乱立　proliferation of stables
- □ 無縁ではない　not unrelated
- □ ランクに応じて　in accordance with the ranking
- □ 相撲協会　Japan Sumo Wrestling Association
- □ 養成費　training fee
- □ 奨励金　subsidy
- □ 財源　financial source
- □ 関取　ranking wrestler

Sumo Wrestling

The number of youths who join up to train to become sumo wrestlers has apparently topped 100 annually. There are nearly 50 sumo wrestling "stables," where the wrestlers live and train; and there's fierce competition between such places to discover new talent, something upon which their very existence depends. The increase in the number of non-Japanese wrestlers has also definitely affected the proliferation of stables. Each of the stables receive training fees and subsidies in accordance with the ranking of its wrestlers from the Japan Sumo Wrestling Association, and this funding becomes the financial source that enables the management of each stable to prosper.

At present, the total number of sumo wrestlers is said to be around 700. Only about 100 can actually make it to the level of *sekitori*, or ranking wrestler, and of these the number of wrestlers who make it to the supreme rank of *yokozuna* is 1 or 2 at the most—such is the fierce competition in the world of sumo.

文化・技芸

大相撲本場所
Grand Sumo Wrestling Official Tournaments

初場所　1月　東京

Hatsu-basho (First Tournament of the Year) January, Tokyo

春場所　3月　大阪

Haru-basho (Spring Tournament) March, Osaka

夏場所　5月　東京

Natsu-basho (Summer Tournament) May, Tokyo

名古屋場所　7月　愛知

Nagoya-basho (Nagoya Tournament) July, Aichi Prefecture

秋場所　9月　東京

Aki-basho (Autumn Tournament) September, Tokyo

九州場所　11月　福岡

Kyūshū basho (Kyūshū Tournament) November, Fukuoka

◁))

番付は、本場所終了3日以内に番付編成会議が開かれ決定する。関取の場合は、**勝ち越し**、**負け越し**1点につき1枚上下するのが原則となっている

The ranking of sumo wrestlers in a particular tournament will have been decided by a special committee within 3 days of the end of the previous tournament. In the case of ranking sumo wrestlers, it's the rule that they move up or down one rank, gaining or losing a rank with successions of victories or defeats.

☐ 番付　the ranking of sumo wrestlers

☐ 勝ち越し　having more wins than losses

☐ 負け越し　having more losses than wins

幕内力士の平均サイズ
The average size of sumo wrestlers

身長183.4cm 体重157.5kg（幕内力士42名、2022年）

Their average height is 183.4 cm; average weight is 157.5 kilos. (42 Makuuchi wrestlers in 2022)

年々、力士の大型化がすすんでいる

The average size is getting bigger every year.

関取（定員70名）には相撲協会から月給が支給され、十両は約110万円、横綱は約300万円。三役（小結、関脇、大関）以上には場所毎に特別手当が付き、横綱は20万円。

Sekitori (70 being the maximum number) receive a monthly salary from the Sumo Association. *Jūryō* wrestlers receive 1,100,000 yen and top-ranking *yokozuna* 3,000,000 yen. *Yokozuna* and the next three ranks—*ōzeki*, *sekiwake*, and *komusubi*—receive a special allowance every tournament, the *yokozuna*'s allowance being 200,000 yen.

優勝
The tournament championship

優勝力士には賞金のほかに、場所によってさまざまな賞品がある

The wrestler who wins a tournament receives prize money, as well as many prizes which vary from region to region.

文化・技芸

新弟子検査

The new apprentice undergoes a check-up to see if he meets the standards.

相撲取りになるには、新弟子検査に合格しなければならない。身長173cm、体重75kg以上必要で、それ以下の人は運動能力テストが課される

To become a sumo wrestler, you must first take the weighing-in test for new apprentices. You must be at least 173 cm tall and weigh 75 kg or more. Anyone not measuring up to these standards are required to take another test for athletic ability.

相撲教習所
（6か月間通う）

Sumo training school
The new apprentice attends for six months.

序ノ口
Jonokuchi: lowest rank

序二段
Jonidan: second-to-lowest rank

三段目
Sandanme: third rank

幕下
Makushita: lower junior grade
sumo wrestler

□ 準ずる equivalent　　　□ 推挙される be recommended　　　□ 横綱審議委員会 Yokozuna Deliberation Council

じゅうりょう い じょう せきとり よ
十両以上は関取と呼ばれ、ランクによって決められた人数の付け人(身の回りの
せわやく おな へ や かい りきし つか
世話役で、同じ部屋の下位の力士)を使うことができる

Wrestlers in the *Jūryō* division and above are called *sekitori*, and according to their rank, they are allowed to have one or more *tsukebito*, that is, a personal attendant, who is a lower-ranking wrestler from the same stable.

じゅうりょう つ びと ふたり
十両 (付け人2人)
Jūryō: junior sumo wrestler (has 2 attendants)

まくうち まえがしら つ びと にん
幕内〈前頭〉 (付け人3人まで)
Makuuchi (as many as 3 attendants)

こ むすび つ びと よにん
小結 (付け人4人まで)
Komusubi (as many as 4 attendants)

せきわけ つ びと にん
関脇 (付け人5人まで)
Sekiwake: second junior champion sumo wrestler (as many as 5 attendants)

おおぜき つ びと にん
大関 (付け人6人まで)
Ōzeki: champion (as many as 6 attendants)

よこづな つ びと にん
横綱 (付け人8人まで)
Yokozuna: grand champion sumo wrestler (as many as 8 attendants)

よこづな おおぜき ば しょれんぞくゆうしょう じゅん せいせき りきし すいきょ よこづな
横綱は、大関で2場所連続優勝かそれに準ずる成績をあげた力士が推挙され、横綱
しんぎ いいんかい しんぎ へ けってい
審議委員会の審議を経て、決定する

Wrestlers who become *yokozuna* must win two grand tournaments in a row as an *ōzeki*, or else have shown equivalent results. They will first be recommended, and the matter will be deliberated by the Yokozuna Deliberation Council, after which a decision will be made.

47

文化・技芸

祇園は一種独特の世界である。特に舞妓の髪型は、日本文化の一断面を覗かせていて興味深い。髪型は、型から入ることを伝統とする日本文化のなかにあっては、ある面では一人の人間の成長過程を表すものであった。舞妓の場合でも、髪型はその娘時代の微妙な移り変わりを物語る。この明治以前からの伝統が、祇園では今なお生き続けているのである。

古き時代の女性と同様、現代女性にとっても髪は女の命である。朝シャンに励む彼女たちにも、その血は流れているのかも知れない。

□髪型 hairstyle
□一断面を覗かせている reflect an aspect
□型から入る on the prerequisite of *kata* (form)
□微妙な移り変わり subtle developments and changes
□命 vital part
□朝シャン daily morning shampoos
□励む assiduously carry out
□その血は流れている the blood runs in the veins

The Rules of Gion

Gion is a special world with its own particular set-up and rules. The hairstyles of *maiko* (apprentice geisha) are particularly interesting, and reflect an aspect of Japanese culture. In Japanese culture, which has long put special emphasis on the prerequisite of *kata* (form), a person's hairstyle can express the particular stage he or she is in during life. The hairstyles of a *maiko* tell a story about the subtle developments and changes that occur as a young girl grows to womanhood. This is a tradition dating from before the Meiji period that is alive and well in Gion.

A woman's hair has always been considered a vital part of her femininity. Perhaps this lies behind the thinking of those contemporary women and girls who assiduously carry out *asa-shan*, daily morning shampoos.

Culture and Arts

文化・技芸

◁))) お茶屋遊びのしくみ
The rules of the teahouse

お茶屋へは、飛び込みでは入れない。
なじみ客や一流旅館などの紹介が必要

You can't just turn up at an *o-chaya* (teahouse) and expect to be served. You must first be introduced by a longtime customer, a first-class *ryokan*, or a traditional inn.

すんません
もうご予約が入って
ますんで……。

Sorry, we are fully booked.

店が空いていても、やんわりと断られる

Even though there are empty rooms, first-time customers are gently turned down.

女将
O-kami
(proprietress of the teahouse)

◁)))

京都市内には、観光客向けに舞妓に変身させてくれる店がたくさんあって、女性に大人気。くれぐれも街を練り歩く舞妓姿に騙されないように！

Popular among women are the Kyoto shops that transform tourists into *maiko*. Don't be fooled by these fake *maiko* parading around the streets!

□お茶屋 teahouse
□飛び込みでは入れない cannot just turn up at and expect to be served
□なじみ客 longtime customer/patron

□練り歩く parade
□口添え introduction
□女将 proprietress
□仕出し屋 caterer

Culture and Arts

正式な紹介のされ方
Formal ways of Introduction

なじみ客に一度紹介してもらう

Get a longtime patron of the o-chaya to introduce you.

O-kami, you remember the fellow I brought along last month...

女将、この前のな……

なじみ客
Longtime patron

おいでやす

Welcome!

なじみ客になるまでは、口添えが必要

You need an introduction to be accepted as a regular customer.

花奴どす

i'm Hanayakko.

舞妓や芸妓は、お茶屋の女将が手配してくれる

The *o-kami* (proprietress) is the one who arranges for *maiko* and geisha to come to the teahouse.

お茶屋では料理はつくらず仕出し屋から取り寄せる

None of the food items are prepared on the premises: they are instead specially ordered from caterers.

217

文化・技芸

舞妓から芸妓へのプロセス
How a *maiko* becomes a *geisha*

お小女さん
Ochobo-san

お仕込さんとも言い、舞妓になる前の見習い期間

Before a girl formally becomes a *maiko*, while she's still learning the basics by observation, she is called *ochobo-san* or *oshikomi-san* ("little learner").

初出し
Debut

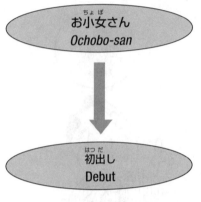

舞妓としての期間はさほど長くはない。舞妓のキャリアは、髪型の変化でわかる

The amount of time she spends as a *maiko* does not last all that long. You can tell what stage a *maiko* is in her apprenticeship by the style in which she wears her hair.

見習い期間が終了すると
いよいよ舞妓としてスタート

Finally, after a long period of practice and observation, the girl makes her debut as a *maiko*.

割りしのぶ
Warishinobu

初出しから1年目くらい

Warishinobu, "divided chignon," worn for about year after her debut

---

- □ 自前の髪 one's own hair
- □ だらりの帯 *obi* which is tied to hang down voluminously
- □ お太鼓 drum-shaped *obi*

The Rules of Gion······3

Culture and Arts

襟替え
Turns her collar

これで一人前になれるのね！

I guess this means I'm finally qualified!

舞妓の時代を終え芸妓になること。自前の髪はかつらになり、だらりの帯はお太鼓に、赤い襟が白い襟に変わる

Once a *maiko* has finished her apprenticeship, she can become a full-fledged geisha. Instead of styling her own hair, she will now wear an ornamental wig. Her *obi* (sash), which previously would have been tied to hang down voluminously in front, will be tied in a much neater knot (called a *taiko*, or "drum") at the back. Her collar, previously red, will now be white.

↑

さっこうまげ
Sakkō

襟替えの数日前から

Sakkō-mage, worn for a few days before the *maiko* "turns her collar"

↑

奴
Yakko

襟替えの1か月前から

Yakko, worn from about one month before the *maiko* "turns her collar"

↑

➡ **おふく**
O-fuku

キャリアを積んだ舞妓の一般的髪型。20歳になると芸妓への道を進む娘も多い

O-fuku, the usual hairstyle for a maiko. Many girls go on to become geisha at the age of 20.

舞妓をめざす少女は中学生の頃から、お茶屋に住み込む。中学を卒業後は八坂女紅場学園に入って、京舞や三味線などの修業を積む

Girls who have decided that they want to become *maiko* take up residence in an *o-chaya* from middle-school age. After graduating from middle-school, they enter the special school to learn traditional performing arts, where they pursue training in dancing the Dances of the Old Capital and playing the *shamisen*.

Read Real NIHONGO

全図解 日本のしくみ
The Complete Guide to Japanese Systems

2023年11月4日　第1刷発行

著　者　安部　直文

訳　者　マイケル・ブレーズ

イラスト　テッド・高橋

発行者　浦　　晋亮

発行所　IBCパブリッシング株式会社
　　　　〒162-0804 東京都新宿区中里町29番3号　菱秀神楽坂ビル
　　　　Tel. 03-3513-4511　Fax. 03-3513-4512
　　　　www.ibcpub.co.jp

印刷所　株式会社シナノパブリッシングプレス

© IBC Publishing, Inc. 2023

Printed in Japan

ISBN978-4-7946-0788-1